NEW VISTAS

Getting Started

STUDENT BOOK

H. DOUGLAS BROWN

ANNE ALBARELLI-SIEGFRIED

FEDERICO SALAS

ALICE SAVAGE • MASOUD SHAFIEI

Longman

Library of Congress Cataloging–in–Publication Data

Brown, H. Douglas, 1941–
    New vistas, getting started / H. Douglas Brown.
         p.   cm.
    ISBN 0–13–908351–0
    1. English language– – Textbooks for foreign speakers.   I.   Title.
PE1128.B7249   1998
428.2'4--DC21   97-44199
                                                CIP

Publisher: *Mary Jane Peluso*
Series Editor: *Stella Reilly*
Development Editor: *Margaret Grant*
Director of Production and Manufacturing: *Aliza Greenblatt*
Production/Design Manager-Multimedia: *Paul Belfanti*
Electronic Production Editor and Realia: *Paula D. Williams*
Production Assistant: *Christine Lauricella*
Electronic Art Production Supervisor: *Ken Liao*
Manufacturing Manager: *Ray Keating*
Art Director: *Merle Krumper*
Cover Coordinator: *Merle Krumper, Eric Dawson*
Illustrators: *Carlotta Tormey, Catherine Doyle Sullivan, Shelly Matheis, Betsy Day*
Realia: *Carey Davies, Steven Greydanus, Michelle LoGerfo, Wendy Wolf*
Interior Design: *Eric Dawson*
Cover Design: *Carmine Vecchio*

© 1999 by Prentice Hall Regents
A Pearson Education Company
Pearson Education
10 Bank Street, White Plains, NY 10606

Printed in the United States of America

10 9 8 7 6 5 4

ISBN 0-13-908351-0

Reviewers

Kathy Broeckel, *College of DuPage;* David Clark, *Fukuoka Kaisei Joshi Gakuin Koto Gakko;* Robert A. Cote, *Lindsey Hopkins Technical Education Center;* Ulysses D'Aquila, *City College of San Francisco;* M. Sadiq Durrani, *BNC Santa Cruz;* Thomas J. Foran, *Fairfield University;* Linda Forse, *University of Texas—Brownsville;* Charles Garcia, *University of Texas—Brownsville;* Sonia Maria Baccari de Godoy, *Uniao Cultural Brasil—Estados Unidos;* Kathleen Huggard Gomez, *Hunter College;* Kathy Hamilton, *Elk Grove Unified School District;* Kevin Keating, *University of Arizona;* Gary Klowak, *Centro internacional de idiomas maestros asociados;* Leigh Manning, *Elk Grove Unified School District;* Rosa Moreno, *Instituto Cultural Peruano—Norte americano;* Betty Otiniano, *Instituto Cultural Peruano—Norte americano;* Herbet D. Pierson, *St. John's University;* Charles Quigley, *El Paso Community College;* John J. Quinn, *Albany Park Community Center;* Alison Rice, *Hunter College;* Maria Vieira, *Yazigi Language Schools, Brasil;* Tammy Smith-Firestone, *Edgewood Language Institute;* Garnet Templin-Imel, *Bellevue Community College*

Contents

Unit	Topics	Functions

1

Meeting People

Meeting People

- Greetings
- Introductions
- Personal Information
- Leave-takings

- Greeting people and responding to greetings
- Introducing yourself and other people
- Exchanging personal information
- Saying good-bye
- Identifying parts of the day

2

Personal Information

Personal Information

- The Alphabet
- Spelling
- Repeating
- Cardinal Numbers
- Address and Phone Number

- Requesting and giving personal information
- Identifying and using alphabet letters and numbers
- Alphabetizing names
- Requesting and giving a spelling
- Expressing a lack of understanding
- Asking someone to repeat
- Repeating something when asked to do so
- Making and responding to a request

- Hello. or Hi.
- Good morning/ afternoon/evening.
- I'm _____. or My name's _____.
- _____, this is _____.
- It's nice to meet you. Nice to meet you, too.
- How are you? I'm fine, thank you. Not too good.
- Good-bye. or Bye.
- Good night. See you tomorrow.

Pronunciation
- **Correctly pronounce words with the short *a* sound.**

Listening
- Listen for the correct intonation in greetings and leave-takings
- Demonstrate understanding of words and phrases learned by correctly using them in appropriate situations

Speaking
- Introduce oneself or someone else
- Greet someone, using words and phrases learned in this unit
- Request information from others in an introduction

- Read and write greetings and simple polite expressions
- Fill in and create simple charts

- What's your full name?
- Spell your first name, please.
- I don't understand. Please repeat.
- Sign here, please. Sure. or OK.

Pronunciation
- **Produce the correct sound of each letter of the alphabet and cardinal numbers**
- **Correctly pronounce words with the short *e* sound**

Listening
- Relate phonological sounds to letters (sound-symbol correspondence)
- Listen for details

Speaking
- Request and give personal information
- Request and give the spelling of a word
- Express a lack of understanding
- Ask someone to repeat
- Give thanks and respond to thanks

- Complete simple charts
- Fill out an identification card
- Indicate first and last names on a registration form

Unit	Topics	Functions

Places in School

Places in School
- The Classroom
- The School
- Directions

- Giving and responding to commands
- Identifying classroom objects
- Correcting wrong information
- Requesting and giving clarification
- Identifying basic school staff and facilities
- Giving and responding to simple directions

4

The Family

The Family
- The Family
- Physical Descriptions

- Identifying family members
- Talking about family
- Requesting information about physical characteristics
- Describing physical characteristics

5

The Time!

The Time
- Time Expressions
- Invitations
- The Calendar
- Schedules
- Daily Routine

- Asking and telling the time
- Naming the days of the week
- Requesting and giving information
- Requesting and giving clarification
- Inviting someone to do something
- Accepting an invitation
- Planning and discussing a schedule

- Please give me that book.
  Sure.
  Here you are.
- Is this the Registrar's Office?
  No, this is the Director's Office.
- Let me see if I understand.
  Excuse me.
- Go straight. Turn left/right.

Pronunciation
- **Correctly pronounce words with the short *I* sound**

Listening
- Demonstrate understanding of simple directions

Speaking
- Give and respond to commands
- Correct wrong information
- Give and respond to directions
- Request and give clarification

- Write simple directions
- Demonstrate understanding of simple written directions
- Create a simple floor plan

- I have two brothers.
  I have a sister.
- What does Judy look like?
  What color is his/her hair?
- He/She's short/tall/average height.

Pronunciation
- **Correctly pronounce words with the short *o* sound**

Listening
- Demonstrate understanding of simple questions

Speaking
- Identify family members orally
- Request and give a physical description

- Read a paragraph
- Read for details
- Complete a chart
- Make a simple family tree
- Write physical descriptions
- Complete a questionnaire

- What time is it, please?
  It's seven thirty-five.
  Excuse me?
  It's twenty-five to eight.
- What time is the party?
  It's at 7:00 P.M.
- Do you want to go to the party?
  I'd love to go.
- I get up at 7:00. I work from 9 to 5.

Pronunciation
- **Correctly pronounce words with the short *u* sound.**

Listening
- Interpreting and responding to verbal messages

Speaking
- Request and tell the time
- Request and give clarification
- Invite someone to do something
- Accept an invitation

- Create a daily schedule
- Read a calendar

Unit	Topics	Functions
6	Review Unit	
7 Money and Shopping	**Money and Shopping** • U.S. Currency • Prices • Shopping	• Identifying U.S. currency by name and value • Requesting and giving prices • Making and responding to a request for specific coins • Making and responding to a request for change
8 Expressing Availability and Abilities	**Expressing Availability and Abilities**	• Requesting and giving addresses • Asking and saying what people can or can't do • Asking for help to locate an address • Inviting someone • Requesting help
9 The House	**The House** • The Home • Furniture • Location • Daily Activities	• Identifying rooms in a house • Identifying furniture and objects in the house • Describing things and their location • Asking and telling what people are doing

- How much is this?
  It's $1.25. *or* It's a dollar.
- How much are the apples?
  They're five for $2.25.
- I need change for a five. Here are four ones, three quarters, two dimes, and a nickel.
- Do you have a dime?
  Yes, I do. Here's ten cents.

Pronunciation
- **Correctly pronounce words with the long *a* sound**

Listening
- Listen for and interpret details in information given verbally
- Respond appropriately to verbal requests

Speaking
- Request and give prices
- Request and give change or specific coins

- Write the names and numerical values of U.S. currency
- Read advertisements
- Read and write prices of goods
- Read and interpret shopping receipts
- Write a shopping list

- Can you dance?
  Yes, I can. *or* No, I can't.
- Can you come to my house tonight?
  No, I can't. How about tomorrow afternoon?
- Excuse me. I can't find number 1314 Spring Street.

Pronunciation
- **Correctly pronounce words with the long *e* sound**

Listening
- Receive and interpret details in information given verbally

Speaking
- Invite someone to do something
- Accept or decline an invitation
- Negotiate times
- Request and give an address or phone number

- Read and write complete sentences

- This is my living room.
- Is there a tree in the yard?
  Yes, there is. / No, there isn't.
  Are there curtains in the living room?
  No, there aren't.
- He's cooking dinner.
  They're setting the table.

Pronunciation
- **Correctly pronounce words with the long *i* sound**

Listening
- Demonstrate understanding of common vocabulary and functions of things used around the house

Speaking
- Describe things and their locations
- Talk about what people are doing

- Label the parts of the house and objects in the house
- Write a description of a house

Unit	Topics	Functions

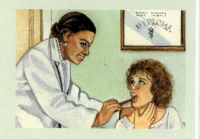

10 Health and the Body

Health and the Body
- Parts of the Body
- Common Illnesses
- Medical Services

- Identifying parts of the body
- Responding to commands and questions from healthcare personnel
- Indicating areas of pain
- Asking how others feel and expressing how one feels
- Filling out and signing forms
- Identifying common medications
- Expressing state of being
- Offering sympathy

11 Colors and Clothes

Colors and Clothes
- Clothes
- Colors
- The Weather
- The Seasons

- Describing what one is wearing
- Talking about the seasons and the weather
- Identifying clothes by their name and color
- Asking for and making a suggestion
- Complimenting and acknowledging a compliment

12

Review Unit

- What's the matter?
  How do you feel?
  Does she have a fever, too?
- I have a cold.
  I feel terrible/ dizzy.
  My throat hurts.
  She has a headache.
  Mia feels sick.
- I am sad/sick/homesick.
- I'm sorry to hear that.
- Don't worry. You'll be fine.
  Breathe in/Breathe out.
  Take an aspirin.

Pronunciation

- **Correctly pronounce words with the long *o* sound**

Listening

- Demonstrate understanding of simple commands given by healthcare personnel
- Demonstrate comprehension of words used for common illnesses

Speaking

- Express state of being
- Ask how someone feels

- Fill out a simple hospital form
- Write a simple note explaining one's absence

- It's a red sweater.
  They're brown pants.
- It's very cold in Chicago in January.
- Do I need my red sweater?
  Yes, and your blue jacket, too.
- What can Oscar wear?
  Oscar can wear _____.
- I like your shirt.
  Thanks. *or* Thank you.
  You're very handsome.

Pronunciation

- **Correctly pronounce words with the long *u* sound**

Listening

- Listen for details
- Demonstrate understanding of words related to colors and clothes

Speaking

- Describe clothes and colors
- Compliment someone
- Respond to a compliment
- Make suggestions

- Write descriptions of clothes

To the Teacher

New Vistas is a series that features the best of what has come to be known as "communicative language teaching," including recent developments in creating interactive, learner-centered curriculum. With *New Vistas,* your students become actively involved in their own language acquisition through collaboration with you as their guide and facilitator.

The Components of *New Vistas*

Student Books

The five-level student books begin with *Getting Started.* Here, students learn basic life skills and vocabulary. Then, in the subsequent levels, students develop their competence and proficiency step by step in all four skills.

Primary features of all the *Student Books* include a storyline with multi-ethnic characters, providing students with opportunities to be personally involved in real-life contexts for learning; a carefully graded series of pronunciation modules; many opportunities for group and pair interaction; listening comprehension exercises; a new and exciting online feature that introduces students to Internet technology; a strategy-awareness section in each unit that stimulates students to reflect on their own preferred pathways to success; and end-of-unit grammar and communication skills summaries.

Teacher's Resource Manuals

For each unit, the *Teacher's Resource Manual* provides an overview of topics, functions, communication skills, and skills standards covered. This is followed by step-by-step, explicit teaching instructions; answer keys for the exercises in the *Student Books* and the *Workbooks,* tapescripts for the listening and pronunciation exercises; grammar activity masters; and placement and achievement tests.

Workbooks

These supplements provide numerous written exercises that reinforce the grammar points and structures taught in the *Student Books. Workbook* exercises are suitable for additional in-class practice or for homework.

The Audio Programs

The audiotapes provide stimulating listening and pronunciation practice that add to the authenticity of classroom pedagogy.

Introduction to the Student

Welcome to *New Vistas*! Today, English is an international language used in every country in the world. It is the language of business, economics, government, education, and tourism virtually everywhere. Learning English will give you the opportunity to participate in worldwide communication across national and linguistic boundaries, and to be a more effective member of tomorrow's international community.

New Vistas is a course in English designed to give you skills in English that will enable you to be a part of this international communicative network. *Getting Started*, which was designed to meet the needs of a beginner in English, will give you basic skills in English conversation (speaking and listening) along with some practice in reading and writing. You will learn English through lively, interesting situations and carefully designed exercises.

The *Student Book, Workbook,* and *Audio Program* will help you to learn English quickly and efficiently. The *Student Book* is the basic book for classroom practice. The *Workbook* provides extra exercises to challenge you. And the *Audio Program* offers you a chance to hear authentic English spoken by native speakers.

Best wishes as you begin this book!

- H. Douglas Brown, Ph.D.
  Professor of English
  Director of the American Language Institute
  San Francisco State University,
  San Francisco, California

Nice to meet you.

 Look at the pictures. Then read and listen.

Tony: Hi. My name's Tony.

Oscar: Hello. I'm Oscar.

Tony: It's nice to meet you.

Oscar: Nice to meet you, too.

Oscar: Tony, this is Lynn.

Tony: It's nice to meet you, Lynn.

Lynn: Nice to meet you, too.

Yumiko: Hi, Lynn. How are you?

Lynn: I'm fine, thank you. And you?

Yumiko: Fine, thanks.

Good morning.

Yumiko: Good afternoon.

TV Anchor: Good evening.

Oscar: Good-bye.

Tony: Bye.

Yumiko: Good night, Lynn.

Lynn: Bye.

Yumiko: See you tomorrow.

Listen. Then practice with your teacher.

Hello.		Good-bye.
Hi.	Good morning.	Good-bye. *or* Bye.
Hello.	Good afternoon.	Good night.
	Good evening.	See you tomorrow.

1 Hi. My name's Tony.

Listen and repeat.

Tony: Hi. My name's *Tony*.

Oscar: Hello. I'm *Oscar*.

Tony: It's nice to meet you, *Oscar*.

Oscar: Nice to meet you, too, *Tony*.

Tony: Where are you from, *Oscar*?

Oscar: I'm from *Spain*.

Pair Practice with a partner. Use your own information.

Walk around the classroom. Introduce yourself to four classmates. Tell them where you're from. Write their names.

1. _____

2. _____

3. _____

4. _____

2 Tony, this is Lynn.

Listen to the examples.

Examples: *Tony*, this is *Lynn*. *She's* from *China*.
Lynn, this is *Tony*. *He's* from *Brazil*.

Then listen to the conversation.

Oscar: *Tony*, this is *Lynn*. *She's* from *China*.

Tony: It's nice to meet you, *Lynn*.

Lynn: Nice to meet you, too.

Work in groups of three. Practice the conversation. Use your own information.

3 Good morning.

▶️ **Listen and repeat. What do you hear?**

Tony: Good morning. I'm Tony.
Oscar: Hi, Tony. My name is Oscar.

Yumiko: Good afternoon. I'm Yumiko.
Neighbor: Hello, Yumiko. My name
   is Mrs. Roberts.

Anchor: Good evening. I'm Heather
   Jackson. Welcome to the
   6 o'clock news.

Guest: Hello. My name is George
   Sterling.

Pair **Practice with a partner.**

Student A: Good _____ . I'm _____ .

Student B: _____ _____ . My name is _____ .

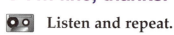 Listen and repeat.

fine   so–so   not too good

Yumiko: Hi, *Lynn*. How are you?

Lynn: I'm *fine*, thank you. And you?

Yumiko: *Fine*, thanks.

Pair Practice the conversation. Use your own information.

5 How about you?

Listen. Check the correct response.

1. _____ Not too good. How about you?   _____ How about you?

2. _____ Fine, thanks.   _____ Hi! How are you?

3. _____ Pretty good, thanks.   _____ Good morning.

4. _____ Yes, thanks.   _____ Fine, thanks.

5. _____ Good afternoon.   _____ Just fine, thanks. How about you?

Greet three other classmates. Ask, "How are you?" Write their names. Then put a check (✓) in the chart under their answers. Tell the class how one classmate feels.

Name	Fine	So–So	Not Too Good
1.			
2.			
3.			

6 Sentence Puzzle, page 97.

Turn to page 97. Work in groups of three or five. Cut out the words, shuffle them, and put them face up on the table. Pick out words to make sentences. Write the sentences on the board.

7 Have a good afternoon.

1. People are saying good-bye. Read the examples.

a. Bye. Have a good afternoon.

b. Good night.

c. Have a good day. See you later.

2. What are they saying? Write *a*, *b*, or *c* under each picture below.

_____   _____   _____

8 See it. Hear it. Say it.

The Sound of Short *a*

Short *a* sounds like the *a* in **cat.**

Listen and repeat.

1. glass	2. map	3. can
4. man	5. lamp	6. fan

CHECKPOINT

I can

- ❑ introduce myself.
- ❑ greet people and respond to greetings.
- ❑ say and respond to simple polite expressions.
- ❑ exchange personal information.
- ❑ say good-bye.
- ❑ identify parts of the day.

VOCABULARY

Greeting and Leave-taking Expressions

Good afternoon.
Good evening.
Good morning.
Good night.
Hello. Hi.

How are you?
Nice to meet you.
See you tomorrow.

Parts of the Day

afternoon
evening
morning
night

► COMMUNICATION SUMMARY

Greeting people
Hello. Hi.
Good morning.
Good afternoon.
Good evening.

Introducing yourself
I'm Oscar.
    My name's Tony.
It's nice to meet you.
    Nice to meet you, too.

Introducing other people
Tony, this is Lynn. She's from China.
    It's nice to meet you, Lynn.
Nice to meet you, too.

Exchanging personal information
How are you?
    I'm fine, thank you. And you?
    Fine, thanks.
    Not too good. How about you?

Saying good-bye
Good-bye. *or* Bye.
Good night.
    See you tomorrow.
    See you later.

UNIT 2
Personal Information

Spell your name, please.

Look at the picture. Then listen and read.

1. Mrs. Brennan
2. Nelson Balewa
3. Yon Mi Lee
4. Yumiko Sato
5. Tony Silva
6. Oscar Garcia
7. Lynn Wang
8. Ivan Gorki

Clerk: What's your full name?
Gina: Gina Poggi.
Clerk: Spell your first name, please.
Gina: G-i-n-a.
Clerk: And your last name?
Gina: P-o-g-g-i.
Clerk: Thank you.

Pair Practice the conversation with a partner.

1 The English Alphabet

🔊 Listen. Say the names of the letters.

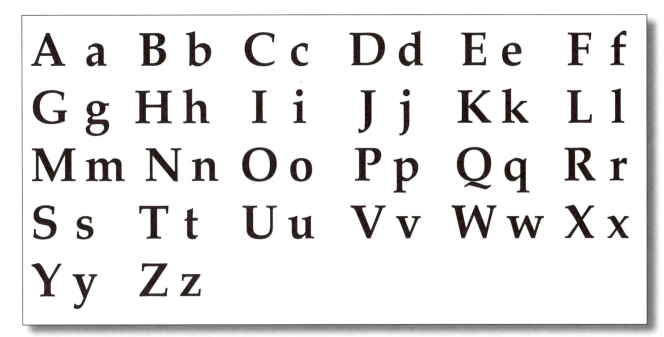

A a   B b   C c   D d   E e   F f
G g   H h   I i   J j   K k   L l
M m   N n   O o   P p   Q q   R r
S s   T t   U u   V v   W w   X x
Y y   Z z

Practice the letters of the alphabet with your teacher.

2 Alphabet Game, page 98.

Group   Turn to page 98. Fill in the grid with 16 letters of the alphabet. Follow your teacher's instructions.

3 Put the names in alphabetical order.

Read the names. Write the names in alphabetical order.

1. Lee   _Balewa_
2. Poggi   _____
3. Balewa   _____
4. Sato   _____
5. Garcia   _____
6. Silva   _____
7. Wang   _____
8. Gorki   _____

Class   Stand up. Arrange yourselves in alphabetical order.

4 It's all in the name.

Look at the picture. Listen to the conversation. Write the missing words.

Librarian: What's your full name?

Michael: Michael Waters.

Librarian: Spell _____ first name, please.

Michael: M-i-c-h-a-e-l.

Librarian: Now _____ your last name.

Michael: W-a-t-e-r-s.

Librarian: What's _____ address?

Michael: 45 Fourth Avenue.

Librarian: What's _____ phone number?

Michael: 555-7853.

5 Sign here, please.

Listen and repeat.

Student A: What's your name?

Student B: (It's) *Gina Poggi*.

Student A: How do you spell your first name?

Student B: *G-i-n-a*.

Student A: And how do you spell your last name?

Student B: *P-o-g-g-i*.

Student A: Sign here, please.

Student B: Sure.

Class Walk around the class. Ask five classmates to spell their names. Write their first names and last names in the chart below. Ask them to sign next to their names.

First Name	Last Name	Signature
Gina	Poggi	*Gina Poggi*

On a piece of paper, put the five last names in alphabetical order.

6 Fill out this form.

Write one letter of your name in each box. Blacken the letters below your name with a pencil.

First Name									Last Name									
A	a	a	a	a	a	a	a	a	A	a	a	a	a	a	a	a	a	a	a
B	b	b	b	b	b	b	b	b	B	b	b	b	b	b	b	b	b	b	b
C	c	c	c	c	c	c	c	c	C	c	c	c	c	c	c	c	c	c	c
D	d	d	d	d	d	d	d	d	D	d	d	d	d	d	d	d	d	d	d
E	e	e	e	e	e	e	e	e	E	e	e	e	e	e	e	e	e	e	e
F	f	f	f	f	f	f	f	f	F	f	f	f	f	f	f	f	f	f	f
G	g	g	g	g	g	g	g	g	G	g	g	g	g	g	g	g	g	g	g
H	h	h	h	h	h	h	h	h	H	h	h	h	h	h	h	h	h	h	h
I	i	i	i	i	i	i	i	i	I	i	i	i	i	i	i	i	i	i	i
J	j	j	j	j	j	j	j	j	J	j	j	j	j	j	j	j	j	j	j
K	k	k	k	k	k	k	k	k	K	k	k	k	k	k	k	k	k	k	k
L	l	l	l	l	l	l	l	l	L	l	l	l	l	l	l	l	l	l	l
M	m	m	m	m	m	m	m	m	M	m	m	m	m	m	m	m	m	m	m
N	n	n	n	n	n	n	n	n	N	n	n	n	n	n	n	n	n	n	n
O	o	o	o	o	o	o	o	o	O	o	o	o	o	o	o	o	o	o	o
P	p	p	p	p	p	p	p	p	P	p	p	p	p	p	p	p	p	p	p
Q	q	q	q	q	q	q	q	q	Q	q	q	q	q	q	q	q	q	q	q
R	r	r	r	r	r	r	r	r	R	r	r	r	r	r	r	r	r	r	r
S	s	s	s	s	s	s	s	s	S	s	s	s	s	s	s	s	s	s	s
T	t	t	t	t	t	t	t	t	T	t	t	t	t	t	t	t	t	t	t
U	u	u	u	u	u	u	u	u	U	u	u	u	u	u	u	u	u	u	u
V	v	v	v	v	v	v	v	v	V	v	v	v	v	v	v	v	v	v	v
W	w	w	w	w	w	w	w	w	W	w	w	w	w	w	w	w	w	w	w
X	x	x	x	x	x	x	x	x	X	x	x	x	x	x	x	x	x	x	x
Y	y	y	y	y	y	y	y	y	Y	y	y	y	y	y	y	y	y	y	y
Z	z	z	z	z	z	z	z	z	Z	z	z	z	z	z	z	z	z	z	z

7 I'm sorry. I don't understand.

Look at the picture on page 8. Listen to the conversations.

Student A:	What's *his* full name?		**Student A:**	What's *her* full name?
Student B:	*Ivan Gorki.*		**Student B:**	*Lynn Wang.*
Student A:	Spell *his* first name, please.		**Student A:**	Spell *her* first name, please.
Student B:	*I-v-a-n.*		**Student B:**	*L-y-n-n.*
Student A:	And *his* last name?		**Student A:**	And *her* last name?
Student B:	*G-o-r-k-i.*		**Student B:**	I'm sorry. I don't understand. Please repeat.
			Student A:	How do you spell *her* last name?
			Student B:	*W-a-n-g.*

Pair Work with a partner and ask questions about the students in the picture on page 8.

Look at the picture above. Listen to the conversation. Write the missing words.

Student A: What's _____*her*_____ name?

Student B: Blanca Torres.

Student A: How do you spell _____ first name?

Student B: B-l-a-n-c-a.

Student A: And her _____ name?

Student B: I'm sorry. I don't understand.

Student A: How do you _____ her last name?

Student B: T-o-r-r-e-s.

8 Let's count.

 Listen and repeat.

Numbers

0	zero (oh)	10	ten	20	twenty	30	thirty
1	one	11	eleven	21	twenty-one	40	forty
2	two	12	twelve	22	twenty-two	50	fifty
3	three	13	thirteen	23	twenty-three	60	sixty
4	four	14	fourteen	24	twenty-four	70	seventy
5	five	15	fifteen	25	twenty-five	80	eighty
6	six	16	sixteen	26	twenty-six	90	ninety
7	seven	17	seventeen	27	twenty-seven	100	one hundred
8	eight	18	eighteen	28	twenty-eight	1000	one thousand
9	nine	19	nineteen	29	twenty-nine		

9 What's your phone number?

 Listen to the conversations. Circle the phone number you hear.

1. a. 212-555-9833   b. 212-555-9823   c. 201-555-9823

2. a. 718-555-5206   b. 973-555-5206   c. 914-555-4206

3. a. 908-555-2002   b. 201-555-2003   c. 212-555-2003

4. a. 914-555-3214   b. 516-555-2314   c. 516-555-3241

10 Fill out the ID cards.

Fill out the card with your own information.

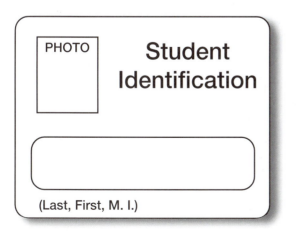

11 What's your address? What's your phone number?

Walk around the class. Ask a few classmates these questions. "What's your name?" "What's your address?" "What's your telephone number?" Write the information in the chart. Ask them to spell the words you don't know.

Names and Addresses	Telephone Numbers
Name:	
Street:	
City:	
Name:	
Street:	
City:	
Name:	
Street:	
City:	

12 Here's my identification card.

Look at these two ID cards. Then answer the questions.

Houston Public Library ID

ID A50387594
Name: John Anderson
Address: 348 Bulk St. Apt. 5B
Houston, TX 77038
Phone (Home): (713) 555-3673
        (Work): (713) 555-7360

Anderson English Institute

ID 02376487
Name: Aiko Mizoi
Address: 9364 Fountain Ave.
San Francisco, CA 94132
Phone: (415) 555-7931

1. What is John Anderson's ID number?

   _____

2. What's his address?

   _____

   _____

3. What's his work number?

   _____

1. What is Aiko's last name?

   _____

2. What's Aiko's address?

   _____

   _____

3. What's her phone number?

   _____

13 Mystery Message

Pair   Find out what the mystery message is. Use the Letter Code to write the message.

23 25 13   1 25   12 25 17   10 2 26 18 18   12 25 17 5   18 7 10 14   4 7 8 26 **?**

___ ___ ___   ___ ___   ___ ___ ___   ___ ___ ___ ___ ___   ___ ___ ___ ___   ___ ___ ___ ___   ___ ___ ___ ___ **?**

8 12   18 7 10 14   4 7 8 26   9 10   24 25 5 15 7.

___ ___   ___ ___ ___ ___   ___ ___ ___ ___   ___ ___   ___ ___ ___ ___ ___ .

Letter Code				
1 = D	6 = J	11 = F	16 = X	21 = K
2 = P	7 = A	12 = Y	17 = U	22 = V
3 = G	8 = M	13 = W	18 = L	23 = H
4 = N	9 = I	14 = T	19 = C	24 = Z
5 = R	10 = S	15 = B	20 = Q	25 = O
				26 = E

14 See it. Hear it. Say it.

The Sound of Short *e*

Short *e* sounds like the *e* in **ten**.

Listen and repeat.

1. bed	2. jet	3. ten
4. men	5. pen	6. desk

CHECKPOINT

I can

❑ ask for and give personal information.

❑ identify and use alphabet letters and numbers.

❑ ask for and give a spelling.

❑ express a lack of understanding.

❑ fill out an identification card.

❑ fill in first and last name on a registration form.

❑ ask someone to repeat.

❑ repeat something when asked to do so.

❑ make and respond to a request.

❑ thank a person and respond to thanks.

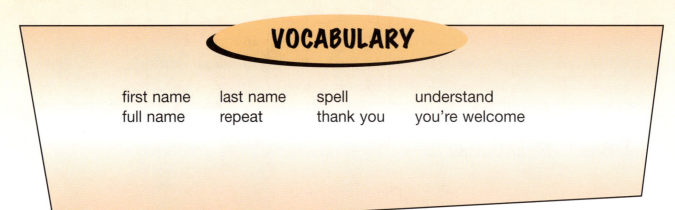

VOCABULARY

first name	last name	spell	understand
full name	repeat	thank you	you're welcome

▶ COMMUNICATION SUMMARY

Requesting and giving personal information
What's your full name?
　Gina Poggi.
What's your telephone number?

Requesting and giving a spelling
Spell your first name, please.
　G-i-n-a.

Expressing a lack of understanding
I don't understand.

Asking someone to repeat
Please repeat.

Giving and responding to directions
Sign here, please.
　Sure. OK.

Thanking and responding to thanks
Thanks. *or* Thank you.
　You're welcome.

UNIT 3
Places in School

The Classroom

Look at the picture. Listen and read.

a clock

a door

a chalkboard

a bookshelf

a window

a printer

a pencil sharpener

an eraser

a keyboard

a monitor

a piece of chalk

a computer

a book

a desk

a chair

a globe

a dictionary

a file cabinet

a pen

a pencil

a notebook

1 Word Bag: The Classroom

Match the words with the pictures. Number the words.

_11_   a chalkboard
_12_   a bookshelf
_8_   a chair
_15_   a piece of chalk
_6_   a clock
_14_   a computer
_13_   a desk
_7_   a dictionary
_10_   an eraser
_2_   a file cabinet
_9_   a globe
_3_   a notebook
_1_   a pencil sharpener
_5_   a window
_4_   a pencil
_16_   a door (closed)

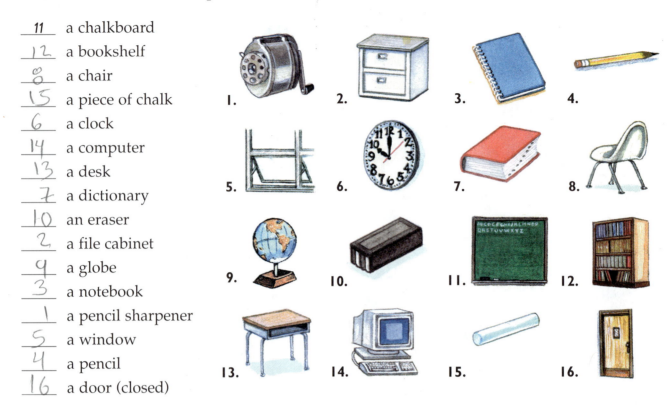

2 Concentration Game, pages 99 and 100.

Turn to pages 99 and 100. Work in groups of three or five. Cut out the word and picture cards. Shuffle the picture cards. Place them, face down, in five rows of four. Do the same for the word cards. Take turns turning over a picture card and a word card. If the two match, read the word and keep the cards. If the cards don't match, put back the cards, face down. The student with the most pairs of matching cards wins.

3 Please turn on the computer.

🔊 Listen to each conversation.

Listen again. Write the missing words. Use words from the box below.

turn on	help	open	give

Mrs. Brennan: Open your book, Gina.
       Gina: This one, Mrs. Brennan?
Mrs. Brennan: No, Gina. That's a notebook.
             Open that book on your left.
       Gina: Oh, this one! What page?
Mrs. Brennan: _____ the book to page 84.

Ivan:	_____ me that book, Yumiko.
Yumiko:	Which book?
Ivan:	The math book, please.
Yumiko:	Sure, Ivan, here you are.
Ivan:	Thank you.

Oscar:	Can you _____ me with my computer, Lynn?
Lynn:	Excuse me?
Oscar:	Please _____ the computer for me.
Lynn:	Sure. It's easy!

Pair Work with a partner. Practice the conversations.

4 Turn on the computer.

Listen. Circle the correct picture.

1. a. 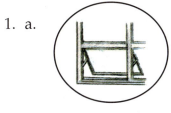   b.

2. a.    b.

3. a.   b.

4. a.   b.

5. a.   b.

5 Is this the Registrar's Office?

Look at the floor plan. Listen to the conversations below.

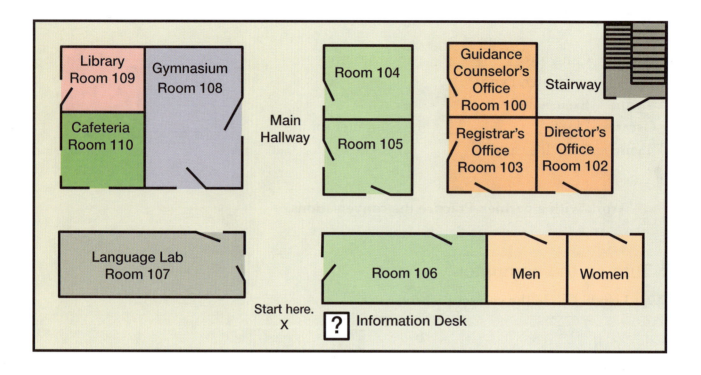

Student A: Is this the Registrar's Office?

Student B: Excuse me?

Student A: Is this the Registrar's Office?

Student B: No, this is the Director's Office. The Registrar's Office is next door.

Student A: Is this Room 106?

Student B: No, it isn't. Room 106 is next to the Men's Room.

Student A: Next to the Men's Room?

Student B: Yes, across the hall from Room 103.

Pair Ask and answer the questions with a partner.

Example: Is the gymnasium across the hall from Room 104?
Yes, it is.

1. Is Room 104 next to the library?

2. Which room is the cafeteria?

3. Is the Language Lab next to the cafeteria?

4. Which room is the Language Lab?

5. Is the Registrar's Office next door to the Guidance Counselor's Office?

6 Where is the gym?

Pair   Look at the map on page 20. Answer the questions.

Example: You are in Room 102. Where is the Registrar's Office?
The Registrar's Office is next door.

1. You're in Room 104. Where is the gym?

2. You're in Room 105. What is next door?

3. You're in the Women's Room. What is across the hall?

4. You're in Room 107. What is across the hall?

7 Where's the library?

Listen to the conversation.

Hakim:	Excuse me, Mrs. Brennan. Where is the library?
Mrs. Brennan:	This is the main hallway. Go straight. Turn left at the next hallway. Go straight to the end. Then turn right at the cafeteria. The library is in Room 109 on the right. It's the big room with glass doors.
Hakim:	Let me see if I understand. Turn left at the next hallway?
Mrs. Brennan:	That's right.
Hakim:	Then turn right at the cafeteria?
Mrs. Brennan:	Yes. The library is down that hallway next to the cafeteria. Look on your right.
Hakim:	Thank you.

1. Turn left.
2. Turn right.
3. Go straight.
4. Go up.
5. Go down.

Pair   Read the conversation again with your partner. Then write a dialog asking how to get to the stairway.

8 Where's the Director's Office?

Listen to the conversations. Follow the directions on the floor plan.

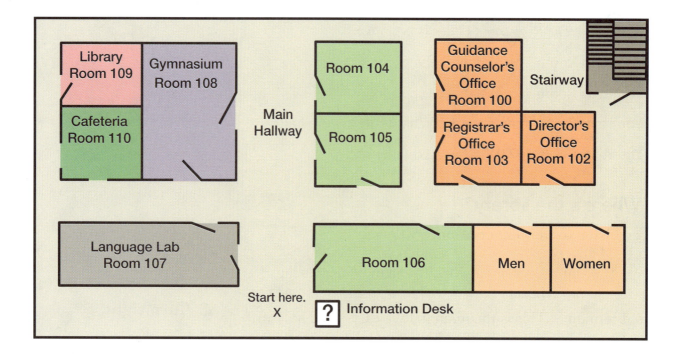

9 It's the door on the left.

Pair   Read the directions and find the room on the floor plan.

Example: Take the main hallway. Go past Room 106 and turn right. Go to the end of the hall. It's the door on the left. Where are you?

    a. the cafeteria

    b. the gymnasium

    c. the Director's Office

1. Take the main hallway. Turn left at the next hallway. It's the door on the left. Where are you?

    a.   the Language Lab

    b.   the cafeteria

    c.   the Men's Room

2. Go to the end of the main hallway. Turn right at Room 104. Go to the end of the hallway. Where are you?

   a. the Guidance Counselor's Office
   b. the stairs
   c. the cafeteria

3. Take the main hallway. Turn right at Room 106. Turn left at the next hallway. Go straight down the hallway. It's the last door on your right. Where are you?

   a. the Guidance Counselor's Office
   b. the stairs
   c. Room 109

4. Take the first left as you go down the main hallway. Go to the end of the hall. Turn right. It's the first door on your right. Where are you?

   a. the Women's Room
   b. the cafeteria
   c. the Language Lab

Pair Give your partner some directions.

10 This is our school.

Group Draw a floor plan of the first floor of your building or school. Show the hallways, the classrooms, the library, the cafeteria, the men's and women's rooms, and the offices.

Pair Choose a "start here" point. Practice giving directions to your partner.

11 See it. Hear it. Say it.

The Sound of Short *i*

Short *i* sounds like the *i* in **six.**

Listen and repeat.

1. fish	2. six	3. pig
4. ship	5. dish	6. gift

CHECKPOINT

I can

❑ give and respond to commands.

❑ identify objects in the classroom.

❑ correct wrong information.

❑ ask for and give clarification.

❑ identify basic school staff and facilities.

❑ give and respond to simple directions.

VOCABULARY

The Classroom	School Facilities and Staff	Directions
chalkboard	cafeteria	Go straight.
book	Director	Take the main hallway.
bookshelf	Guidance Counselor	It's across the hall from
chair	gymnasium (Gym)	Room 105.
chalk	Language Lab	Go to the end of the hallway.
clock	library	Go past Room 106.
computer	Main Hallway	Go up/down.
desk	Men's Room	It's next door.
dictionary	office	Turn left/right.
door	Registrar	Look on your right.
eraser	stairway	It's next to Room 102.
file cabinet	Women's Room	It's the door on the left.
globe		Take the first left.
notebook		
pen		
pencil		
pencil sharpener		
window		

► COMMUNICATION SUMMARY

Giving and responding to commands

Please give me that book.

　　Sure.

　　Here you are.

Correcting information

Is this the Registrar's Office?

　　No, this is the Director's Office.

Requesting and giving clarification

Let me see if I understand . . .

Excuse me?

Giving and responding to directions

Go straight.

Turn left/right.

The Family

This is my family.

Look at the picture. Tommy is talking about his family. Listen.

This is my family.

That's my father, Fred, and this is my mother, Juana.

My grandparents are from Colombia. Now they live here with us.

My grandmother's name is Elsa, and my grandfather's name is Tomas.

This is my sister, Teresa.

My name is Tommy, Tommy Bonilla.

Pair Read the sentences aloud with a partner.

1 Word Bag: The Family

Look at the pictures of Tommy's family. Then listen and read along.

TOMMY'S FAMILY

Fred	Juana	Teresa	Tommy

husband **father**	**wife** **mother**	**daughter** **sister**	**son** **brother**

This is Tommy Bonilla's family.

This is Tommy's father. His name is Fred.

This is Tommy's mother. Her name is Juana.

Teresa is Tommy's sister.

Tommy is Teresa's brother.

Fred and Juana are married.

Fred is Juana's husband, and Juana is Fred's wife.

Teresa is Juana's and Fred's daughter.

Tommy is Juana's and Fred's son.

Listen to the sentences again. Point to each person.

2 Tommy and Teresa are brother and sister.

Pair Look again at the pictures of Tommy's family. Read the sentences. Check (✔) *True* (Yes) or *False* (No).

		True	False
1.	Juana is Tommy's sister.	_____	✔
2.	Tommy is Teresa's brother.	_____	_____
3.	Tommy is Fred's father.	_____	_____
4.	Juana is Fred's wife.	_____	_____
5.	Tommy and Fred are brothers.	_____	_____
6.	Juana is Teresa's mother.	_____	_____
7.	Fred and Juana are husband and wife.	_____	_____
8.	Teresa is Fred's sister.	_____	_____
9.	Juana is Tommy's daughter.	_____	_____
10.	Tommy is Fred's son.	_____	_____

3 What letters are missing?

Write the missing letters.

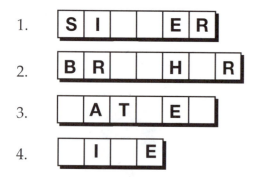

1. `S` `I` ` ` `E` `R`
2. `B` `R` ` ` `H` `R`
3. ` ` `A` `T` `E` ` `
4. ` ` `I` ` ` `E`

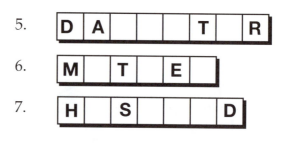

5. `D` `A` ` ` ` ` `T` `R`
6. `M` ` ` `T` ` ` `E` ` `
7. `H` ` ` `S` ` ` ` ` `D`

4 George is Nelson's brother.

Look at Nelson's family. Write one of the family words on each line.

grandfather
grandmother
father
mother
sister
brother
husband
wife
son
daughter

Complete these sentences. Use words from the list above.

1. Samuel is John's _____father_____.
2. Ami is John's _____.
3. Kenisha is Ami's _____.
4. John is George's _____.
5. Kenisha is Nelson's _____.
6. Dora is Nelson's _____.
7. Samuel is Nelson's _____.
8. Nelson is John's _____.

Pair   Compare your answers with a partner.

28   UNIT 4

5 Here's my family.

Bring pictures of your family to class. Paste a picture of each member of your family below.

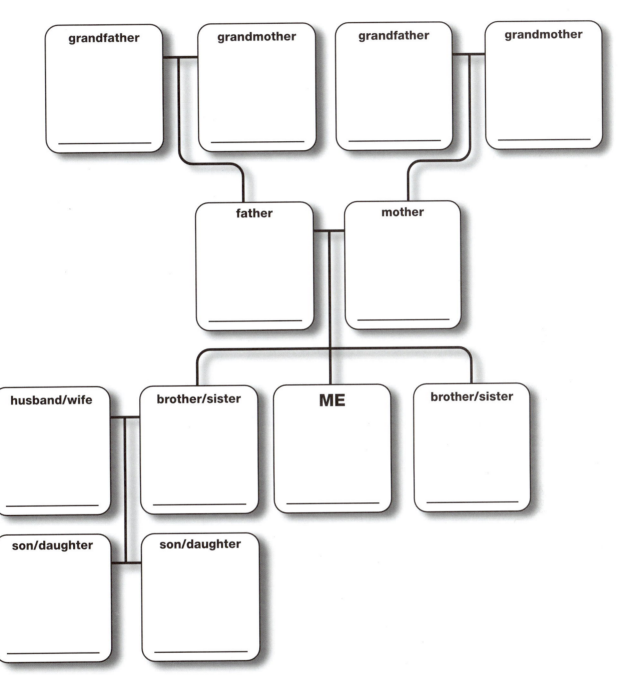

Pair   Work with a partner. Take turns asking and answering questions about your families.

Example: **Student A:** Who's that?
            Student B: That's my *brother*.
            Student A: What's *his* name?
            Student B: *Mario.*

6 What does she look like?

Look at the pictures and read.

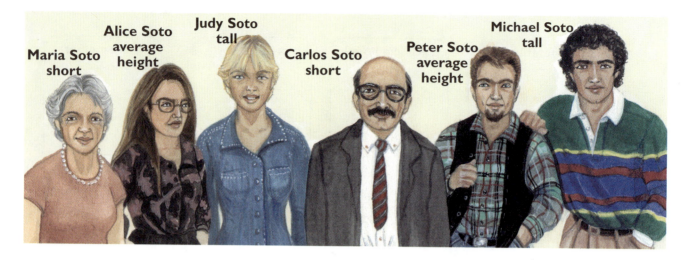

Maria Soto short — Alice Soto average height — Judy Soto tall — Carlos Soto short — Peter Soto average height — Michael Soto tall

🔊 Listen. Write the name of each person on the line as you listen to the cassette.

short blond hair blue eyes	brown hair green eyes	long straight brown hair gray eyes	black curly hair brown eyes	bald brown eyes a mustache
_____	_____	_____	_____	_____

Alice has long brown hair and gray eyes. She's average height.

Carlos is bald. He has brown eyes and a mustache. He's short.

Judy has short blond hair and blue eyes. She's tall.

Michael has black curly hair and brown eyes. He's tall.

Peter has brown hair, green eyes, and a beard. He's average height.

7 Peter is average height.

🔊 Look at the pictures above. Listen to the conversation.

Student A: What does *Judy* look like?

Student B: *She's tall. She* has *short blond hair and blue eyes.*

Student A: What does *her brother,* Peter, look like?

Student B: *Peter* is *average height. He* has *brown hair, green eyes, and a beard.*

Pair Ask and answer questions about your classmates.

8 I have black hair.

Paste a picture of yourself in the space below. Write the missing words. Use your own information.

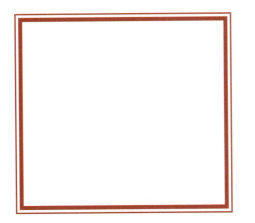

Here I am. I am _____ (height).

I have _____ _____ hair. (color, length)

My eyes are _____ (color).

Now exchange books with a partner. Write the missing words about your partner.

(_____) is _____ (height).

He/She has _____ _____ hair.

Her/His eyes are _____.

Describe your partner to the class.

Paste a picture of a brother or sister or best friend in this space. Write the missing words.

This is my _____.

He/She is _____ (height).

He/She has _____ _____ hair.

His/Her eyes are _____.

Class   Show the picture to your classmates. Describe the person.

9 What color is her hair?

Look at the pictures. Answer the questions on the lines provided.

1. What color is her hair?

_____

2. What color are his eyes?

_____

3. Does he have a mustache?

_____

4. What color is her hair?

_____

5. Does he have a beard?

_____

6. Is her hair long or short?

_____

10 Information Gap Activity, pages 101 and 102.

Turn to pages 101 and 102. Follow your teacher's instructions.

11 Family survey

Group   Work in groups of four. First, write your own information in the questionnaire.
Then ask one another these questions. Complete the questionnaire.

- Are you married/single?
- How many brothers/sisters do you have?
- How many people are there in your family?

Name	Married/ Single	Number of Brothers	Number of Sisters	Total Number of Family Members

QUESTIONNAIRE

Complete this paragraph with information from the questionnaire.

_____ people in our group are married. _____ people in our group are single. Our group has _____ sisters. Our group has _____ brothers. Our group has a total of _____ sisters and brothers.

12 See it. Hear it. Say it.

Read and learn.

The Sound of Short _o_

> **Short _o_ sounds like the _o_ in hot.**

 Listen and repeat.

1. hot
2. box
3. sock
4. stop
5. block
6. fox

CHECKPOINT

I can

❑ identify immediate family members.

❑ talk about immediate family.

❑ ask for a description of a person.

❑ describe a person.

VOCABULARY

Family Members
brother
daughter
father
grandfather
grandmother
husband
mother
sister
son
wife

Physical Characteristics
bald
beard
black hair
blond
blue eyes
brown eyes
brown hair
curly hair
mustache

gray eyes
green eyes
long hair
short
short hair
straight hair
tall

► COMMUNICATION SUMMARY

Talking about family
I have two brothers.
I have a sister.

Requesting information about physical characteristics
What does Judy look like?
What color is his/her hair?

Describing physical characteristics
He's/She's short/tall/average height.

What time is the party?

Look at the picture. Then listen as you read the conversation.

Oscar: There's a party at the Student Center tonight. Do you want to go?
Lynn: What kind of party?
Oscar: Potluck.
Lynn: And what time is the party?
Oscar: It's at 7:00.
Lynn: I'd love to go. Thanks.
Oscar: Great. See you at seven then.

1 Word Bag: The Time

Look at the pictures. Then listen and repeat.

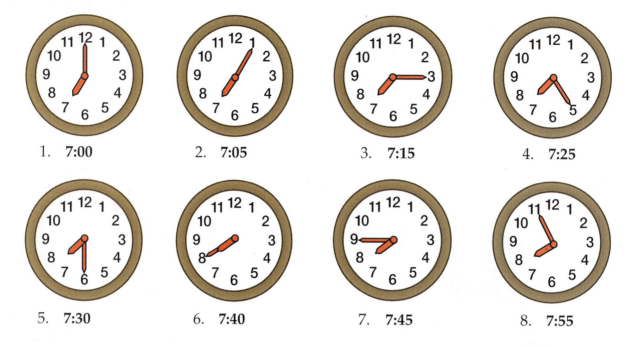

1. 7:00   2. 7:05   3. 7:15   4. 7:25

5. 7:30   6. 7:40   7. 7:45   8. 7:55

Listen and write the time.

1. _____

2. _____

3. _____

4. _____

2 What time is it?

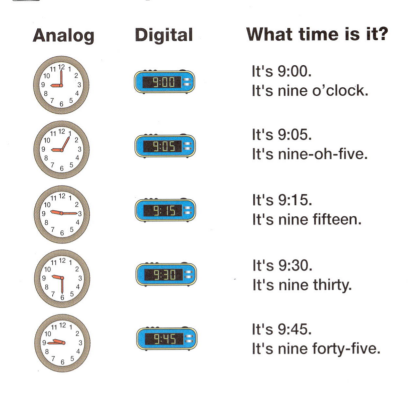

🎧 Listen and repeat.

Analog	Digital	What time is it?
	9:00	It's 9:00. It's nine o'clock.
	9:05	It's 9:05. It's nine-oh-five.
	9:15	It's 9:15. It's nine fifteen.
	9:30	It's 9:30. It's nine thirty.
	9:45	It's 9:45. It's nine forty-five.

3 Information Gap Activity, pages 103 and 104.

Turn to pages 103 and 104. Follow your teacher's instructions.

4 Excuse me?

🎧 Listen.

Student A: What time is it, please?
Student B: It's *seven thirty-five.*
Student A: Excuse me?
Student B: It's *twenty-five to eight.*
Student A: Oh, thanks.
Student B: No problem.

Pair Practice the conversation with your partner. Use the information below.

3:20   10:15   6:30   2:45   10:55

5 You're invited!

🎧 Look at the posters. Then listen. Write the number of the conversation under each picture.

YOU'RE INVITED!
Saturday, 10:30 A.M.

_____

It's time for BASKETBALL
Watch the game!
Saturday 8:00 P.M.

_____

FREE ROCK CONCERT at the park
Join the fun.
Sunday 4:00 P.M. to 12 midnight.

_____

Do you want to learn English FAST?
Come to my class.
Saturdays 12:00 noon

_____

PLANE DEPARTURES

| New York | Sunday, 2:35 P.M. |

_____

Free Movie
at the Student Union every Friday
This week see
STAR WARS
Showtime: 8:00 P.M.

_____

6 The English class is at noon.

Read the posters again. Write the time answer for each question.

at midnight	in the afternoon	in the evening
at night	in the morning	at noon

1. What time is the party?
   In the morning

2. What time is the rock concert?
   at afternoon to midnight.

3. What time is the basketball game?
   in the evening.

4. What time is the movie?
   at night.

5. What time is the plane for New York?
   in the afternoon.

6. What time is the English class?
   at noon.

7 What day is it?

Listen and repeat.

NOVEMBER

Sunday	Monday	Tuesday	Wednesday	Thursday	Friday	Saturday
				1	2	3
4	5	6	7	8	9	10

Fill in the calendar. Write the days of the week.

MARCH

Sunday	Monday	Tuesday	Wednesday	Thursday	Friday	Saturday
Rock concert New york		1	2	3	4 Free movie	5 Poetry 10:30 Am Basketball Learn English
6	7	8	9	10	11	12

Write the activities from the posters on the calendar.

8 It's open Saturdays from 9 to 12.

Look at the sign. Write the missing words.

POST OFFICE	
BUSINESS HOURS	
MONDAY	9:00 – 5:00
TUESDAY	9:00 – 5:00
WEDNESDAY	9:00 – 5:00
THURSDAY	9:00 – 5:00
FRIDAY	9:00 – 5:00
SATURDAY	9:00 – 12:00
SUNDAY	CLOSED

The post office opens at ____9:00 morning____

It closes at 5:00 on _Monday, Tuesday_
_wednesday Thu____, and _Friday_.

It closes at noon on _Saturday_.

It's closed on _Sunday____.

9 What's your schedule?

Read the activities below. Plan your day. Write the day's activities in the schedule below. Share your schedule with the class.

wake up

eat breakfast/lunch/dinner

go to school/work

watch TV

study

go to bed

23 SEPTEMBER		**MONDAY**	
7:00 A.M.	Wake up	3:00	
8:00	eat breakfash	4:00	
9:00	go to work	5:00	
10:00		6:00	Study
11:00		7:00	
12:00 P.M.	lunch	8:00	dinner
1:00		9:00	watch t.v
2:00		10:00	go to bed

10 What a busy week!

First, fill in the names of the days at the top of the calendar, and write the name of a month on the line at the top of the calendar page. Then listen to the conversation.

Sunday	Monday	Tuesday				
		1 2:00 p.m. doctor's appt.	2	3	4 1:30 p.m. class party	5 12:00 English class
6 4:00 p.m. rock concert	7 5:00 p.m. play soccer	8	9 8:00 a.m. dentist's appt.	10	11	12
13	14	15	16	17	18	19 10:30 a.m. kid's party
20	21	22	23	24	25 8:00 p.m. movie	26 8:00 p.m. basketball game
27	28	29	30			

Now ask and answer questions with your partner using the information on the calendar.

Student A: When is your *doctor's appointment?*   **Student B:** It's at *2:00 P.M. on Tuesday.*

11 See it. Hear it. Say it.

Read and learn.

The Sound of Short *u*

> **Short *u*** sounds like the *u* in **sun.**

Listen and repeat.

1. sun	2. cup	3. bus
4. duck	5. brush	6. bug

CHECKPOINT

I can

- ❏ ask for and tell the time.
- ❏ name the days of the week.
- ❏ ask for and give information.
- ❏ ask for and give clarification.
- ❏ invite someone to do something.
- ❏ plan and discuss my schedule.
- ❏ accept an invitation.

VOCABULARY

Daily Routine
wake up
eat breakfast, lunch, dinner
go to school/work
watch TV
study
go to bed

Time Expressions
midnight
night
noon
o'clock
week

Other Words
busy
rock concert
game
movie
potluck party

Days of the Week

Monday	Friday
Tuesday	Saturday
Wednesday	Sunday
Thursday	

▶ COMMUNICATION SUMMARY

Requesting and telling the time
What time is it, please?
   It's nine o'clock.

Requesting and giving clarification
What time is it, please?
   It's seven thirty-five.
Excuse me?
   It's twenty-five to eight.

Requesting and giving information
What time is the party?
   It's at 7:00.

Inviting someone
There is a party at the Student Center tonight.
Do you want to go?

Planning/Discussing a schedule
When is your doctor's appointment?
It's at 2:00 P.M. on Tuesday.

Accepting an invitation
I'd love to go.

UNIT 6
Review of Units 1-5

▶ Topics

Introductions, greetings, leave-takings
The alphabet
Spelling names
Personal information
Places in school
Rooms in the school
Directions
The family
Physical descriptions
Cardinal numbers
Telling time
The calendar
Schedules
Daily routine

▶ Communication Summary

Introducing people
Asking for and giving personal information
Making or responding to a request
Giving and responding to simple directions
Identifying school facilities
Identifying immediate family members
Talking about immediate family
Asking for and giving a description of a person
Asking for and telling the time
Planning and discussing a schedule

Is this the Student Center?

 **Look at the pictures. Then listen and read.**

Oscar:	Excuse me. Is this the Student Center?
Student:	Yes, it is.
Oscar:	Thanks.
Lynn:	Look. There's Yumiko.
Yumiko:	Oscar, Lynn! Over here! I'd like you to meet Maria Pavese. She's a new student.

Oscar:	Nice to meet you, Maria.
Maria:	Nice to meet you, too, Oscar.
Lynn:	Where are you from, Maria?
Maria:	Slovenia. What about you?
Oscar:	I'm from Madrid. And Lynn's from Beijing.

Class With your partner, on your class map or globe, find Slovenia on the map of Europe. Tell the class where Slovenia is.

1 Class Journal

Pair   Work with a partner. Ask him/her the following questions.

Student Questionnaire

1. What day is today? _____
2. How many students are in your class? _____
3. What's your name? _____
4. Where are you from? _____
5. Are you married or single? _____
6. How many brothers do you have? _____
7. How many sisters do you have? _____
8. What color is your hair? _____
9. What color are your eyes? _____

Write about your partner.

Journal

_____ [1]

I am in _____ 's class. There are _____
(teacher's name) [2]

students in my class today. My partner's name is _____ .
[3]

She's/He's from _____ . She/He has _____
[4] [5]

brothers and _____ sisters. My partner has _____
[6] [7]

hair and _____ eyes.
[8]

Read your journal entry to the class.

2 Numbers

Group   Work in groups of five. Write number answers to the questions below. Beside each number, write the word for that number.

Class Survey

Questions

1. How many students are there? _25 twenty-five_
2. How many male students are there? _____
3. How many female students are there? _____
4. How many have brown hair? _____
5. How many have blond hair? _____
6. How many have black hair? _____
7. How many have straight hair? _____
8. How many have curly hair? _____
9. How many have long hair? _____
10. How many have short hair? _____
11. How many have a mustache? _____
12. How many have blue eyes? _____
13. How many have brown eyes? _____
14. How many have green eyes? _____
15. How many are tall? _____
16. How many are short? _____

On a piece of notebook paper, write the names of the members of your group. Below each name, list words that describe the person. Compare notes with your group. Write a group list and description of each person in your group. Have one member read the names and the descriptions.

3 Classroom Commands

Listen to your teacher as he/she reads the directions below. Follow them step-by-step.

1. **Think** of a command, for example, **"Open the door."**
2. **Write** the command on a piece of paper.
3. **Fold** your paper.
4. **Put** your folded paper in a box on your teacher's table.
5. **Pick** another paper from the box.
6. **Read** the command.
7. **Perform** the command.

4 Where are you?

Pair   With a partner, read and follow the directions on the school floor plans below.

School First Floor Plan

Turn left at hallway B. Go past Room 101 and turn left. Go straight and when you reach hallway A, turn right. Go past the Director's Office. It's the next door on the left. Where are you?

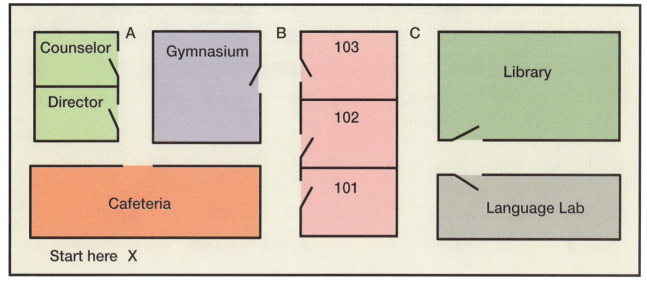

School Second Floor Plan

Turn right at hallway B. Go past Room 202 and turn left. Go past the cafeteria and turn left again. It's the first door on the right. Where are you?

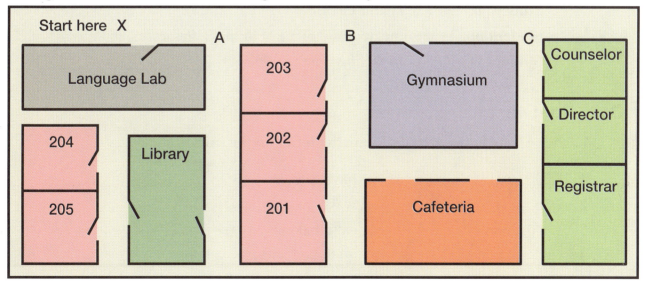

Pair   With your partner, write directions for the class to follow. Read your directions aloud to the class. Tell the students to follow your directions on the First Floor Plan or the Second Floor Plan.

5 The Time

Look at the schedules below. Then listen and repeat.

INTERCONTINENTAL AIRPORT

ARRIVALS	
Paris	10:30 A.M.
Cancun	11:00 A.M.
London	1:00 P.M.
Bogota	2:15 P.M.
Singapore	3:35 P.M.

DEPARTURES	
Madrid	8:25 A.M.
Mexico City	9:45 A.M.
Rome	4:09 P.M.
Buenos Aires	5:17 P.M.
Tokyo	6:50 P.M.

Complete the sentences. Use information from the schedules.

1. The plane from Paris arrives at _____.

2. The plane to Madrid leaves at _____.

3. The plane to Rome leaves at _____.

4. The plane from Singapore arrives at _____.

5. The plane to Buenos Aires leaves at _____.

6. The plane from Bogota arrives at _____.

7. The plane to Tokyo leaves at _____.

8. The plane from Cancun arrives at _____.

9. The plane to Mexico City leaves at _____.

10. The plane from London arrives at _____.

Pair Ask and answer questions about the arrivals and departures.

Student A: What time does the plane *from Paris arrive*?

Student B: *At 10:30 in the morning.*

Student A: What time does the plane *to Buenos Aires leave*?

Student B: *At 5:17 in the afternoon.*

6 Daily Routine

Pair Match the time to the activity. Write the letter on the line.

_b_ 1. 6:30 A.M.   a. have dinner

_c_ 2. 7:30 A.M.   b. wake up

_e_ 3. 12:00 noon   c. eat breakfast

_a_ 4. 6:00 P.M.   d. go to bed and read a book

_f_ 5. 7:00 P.M.   e. have lunch and take a walk

_d_ 6. 10:00 P.M.   f. study

7 Weekly Schedule

Read Oscar's schedule. Complete the sentences below.

Oscar's Schedule						
Sunday	**Monday**	**Tuesday**	**Wednesday**	**Thursday**	**Friday**	**Saturday**
visit grandparents	study English	go to the supermarket	watch TV	study English	go to the movies	play basketball

1. Oscar goes to the supermarket on _Tuesday_ .

2. He studies English on _____ and _____ .

3. He plays basketball on _____ .

4. He watches TV on _____ .

5. He visits his grandparents on _____ .

6. He goes to the movies on _____ .

8 Group Survey

Group Work in groups of four. Ask and answer the following questions. Check *Yes, No,* or *Sometimes.*

Do you . . .	Yes	No	Sometimes
1. wake up late on Sundays?	_____	_____	✓
2. go to the mall on Saturday afternoon?	_____	✓	_____
3. study late in the evening?	_____	_____	✓
4. go to the movies on Friday evenings?	_____	✓	_____
5. work/go to school on the weekends?	_____	_____	✓

Share the information about your group's schedules with the class.

1. _____ member (members) of our group wakes up (wake up) late on Sundays.

2. _____ shop (shops) on Saturday afternoons.

3. _____ study (studies) late in the evening.

4. _____ go (goes) to the movies on Friday evenings.

5. _____ work (works) or go (goes) to school on the weekends.

UNIT 7
Money and Shopping

How much is this?

Look at the picture. Then listen and read.

Oscar:	Excuse me.
Clerk:	Yes. Can I help you?
Oscar:	How much is this?
Clerk:	It's $1.25.
Oscar:	And is this only one dollar?
Clerk:	Yes, it is.
Oscar:	I'll take this one, please.

Pair   Practice the conversation with a partner.

1 Word Bag: Coins

Look at the pictures. Listen and repeat.

		What You Say	What You Write
1.		a penny *or* one cent	$0.01 *or* 1¢
2.		a nickel *or* five cents	$0.05 *or* 5¢
3.		a dime *or* ten cents	$0.10 *or* 10¢
4.		a quarter *or* twenty-five cents	$0.25 *or* 25¢
5.		a half-dollar *or* 50 cents	$0.50 *or* 50¢

Listen to the conversation.

Student A: Do you have *10 cents*?
Student B: *Ten cents*?
Student A: Yes, I need *ten cents*.
Student B: OK. Here's *a dime*.

Pair Practice with a partner. Use the amounts above.

2 Money

Look at the pictures. Listen and repeat.

		You Say	You Write
1.		a dollar *or* one dollar	$1.00
2.		a five-dollar bill *or* five dollars	$5.00
3.		a ten-dollar bill *or* ten dollars	$10.00
4.		a twenty-dollar bill *or* twenty dollars	$20.00
5.		a check	
6.		a credit card	

Listen to the conversation.

Student A: Do you have *a dollar bill*?

Student B: *A dollar bill*?

Student A: Yes, I need *a dollar bill*.

Student B: OK. Here's *a one-dollar bill*.

Pair   Practice with a partner. Use the amounts above.

3 That's $12.60.

Count the money. Circle the total amount.

1. **$1.25**   **$1.10**

2. **$3.25**   **$3.15**

3. **$0.82**   **$0.72**

4. **$8.15**   **$6.30**

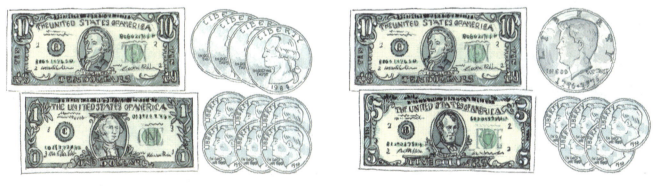

5. **$11.30**   **$12.60**

6. **$15.25**   **$16.00**

🔊 **Listen to the conversation.**

Student A: I need change for a *five-dollar bill*.
Student B: Here are *four ones, three quarters, two dimes, and a nickel*.

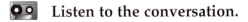 **Pair**   With a partner, use your own currency to practice asking for and giving change.

4 How much is this?

Look at the items for sale. Listen and read.

CABBAGE — 39¢ lb.
ZUCCHINI — $1.99 lb.
ORANGES — 5 for $1.00
APPLES — 89¢ lb.
CARROTS — $1.29 bunch
ONIONS — 2 lbs. for 79¢
GRAPES — $1.49 lb.
PLUMS — $1.49 lb.
BROCCOLI — $1.49 bunch
POTATOES — 49¢ lb.
PINEAPPLES — $1.99 each
BANANAS — 39¢ lb.

Pair   Ask your partner about the price of each item.

Student A: How much is *the cabbage*?
Student B: It's *39 cents a pound*.
Student A: How much are *the potatoes*?
Student B: *They're 49 cents a pound*.

5 It's on sale for $1.29 a pound.

Group Read the supermarket ad. Help Oscar shop for the party.

SALE!

Chicken legs
Only $1.29 a pound

Bananas
5 for 99¢

Potato Chips $1.59 a bag
Corn Chips 99¢ a bag

POTATO CHIPS   CORN CHIPS

Ice Cream all flavors
$2.50 a half gallon

HAPPY COW
Ice Cream
1/2 Gal

Grapes
$1.99 a pound

Cookies
$2.19 a bag

CHOCOLAND Cookies

Butter
$1.99 a pound

HAPPY COW BUTTER
4 sticks
1 lb
Limit 2

Party Mix
$1.50 a bag

PARTY MIX

Hot Dogs
99¢ a package

Hot Dogs

Soda 12-pack
$1.99

COLA

Limit 2
with coupon

Cake Baked on site
$8.99

Happy Birthday

Hot Dog Buns
89¢ a package

Hot Dog Buns

Make a shopping list for Oscar.

Food	Quantity	Price per Item	Total Cost per Item
grapes	___ pound(s)	_____	
soda	___ 12-pack(s)	_____	
cookies	___ bag(s)	_____	
hot dogs	___ package(s)	_____	
buns	___ package(s)	_____	
		Total:	

6 Let's go shopping!

Group   Work in a group of four students. Pretend your group is having a party. There are ten guests. Look at the prices in the ads on page 55 and make a shopping list.

Food	Quantity	Price per Item	Total Cost per Item
			Total:

7 Check your receipts carefully!

Pair   Look at the prices in the ads on page 55. Read the prices on the receipt below. There are three mistakes. Correct the mistakes and add up the new total. Write the correct total.

```
        SPEEDY MART

GRAPES        1 lb.      1.99
SODA          12 PACK    1.90
HOT DOGS      1 PACK      .99
HOT DOG BUNS  2 PACKS    1.50
COOKIES       1 BAG      2.00

TOTAL                    8.38
```

If you give the clerk a $50 dollar bill, what's your change? _____

8 Information Gap Activity, pages 105 and 106.

Turn to pages 105 and 106. Follow your teacher's instructions.

9 See it. Hear it. Say it.

Read and learn.

The Sound of Long *a*

Long *a* sounds like the *a* in **train** and **pay.**

📼 **Listen and repeat.**

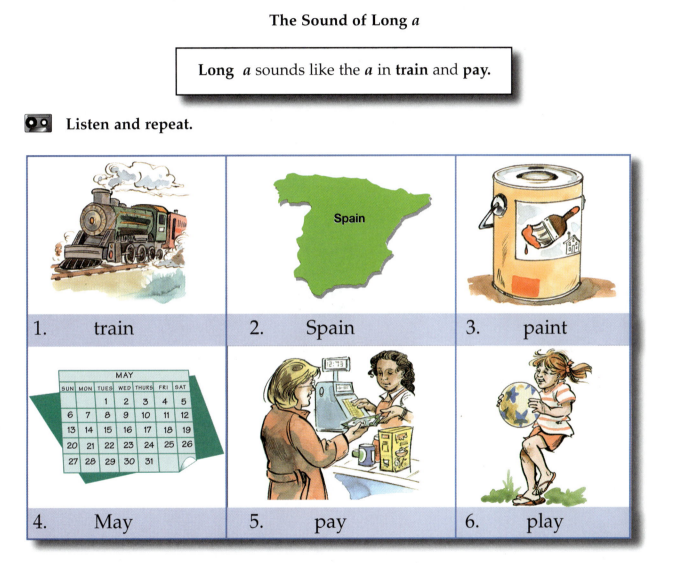

1. train	2. Spain	3. paint
4. May	5. pay	6. play

CHECKPOINT

I can
❑ identify United States coins and bills by name and value.

❑ ask for and give prices.

❑ ask for and give specific coins.

❑ ask for and give change.

VOCABULARY

Money Words
add
change
coin
coupon
total

Shopping Words
ad
buy
go shopping
How much?
sale
supermarket

U.S. Currency
cent
penny
nickel
dime
quarter
half-dollar
dollar
1 dollar
5 dollars
10 dollars
20 dollars
50 dollars

Grocery Shopping

Fruit
apples
bananas
grapes
oranges
pineapples
plums

Vegetables
broccoli   onions
cabbage   potatoes
carrots   zucchini

Other Food Items
butter   hot dogs
cake   hot dog buns
chicken legs   ice cream
cookies   party mix
corn chips   potato chips
                soda

▶ COMMUNICATION SUMMARY

Requesting and giving prices
How much is this?
    It's $1.25 (one twenty-five).
    It's $5 (five dollars).
How much are the apples?
    They're five for $2.25.

Making and responding to a request for change
I need change for a five.
    Here are four ones, three quarters, two dimes, and a nickel.

Making and responding to a request for specific coins
Do you have a dime?
    Yes, I do.
    Here's a dime.

Expressing Availability and Abilities

Can you come to my house tonight?

Look at the picture. Listen and read.

Hi, everyone,
   Let's study English together. Can you come to my house tonight?
   Oscar

Oscar,
   Great idea! Sure I can.
   Yumiko

Oscar and everyone,
   I can't come tonight. What about tomorrow?
   Tony

Oscar and everyone,
   I can come tonight or tomorrow. What's your address and phone number?
   Lynn

Hello, everyone,
   Tony can't come tonight. How about tomorrow afternoon?
   My address is 1314 Spring Street. My phone number is 555-2312.
   Oscar

Read the e-mail again. Answer these questions.

Who can come tonight?
Who can come tomorrow?

1 We can study together.

Listen to the phone calls from Oscar's friends. Who can come to Oscar's house tomorrow?

Lynn	☒ can come	☐ can't come	☒ afternoon	☐ late afternoon
Yumiko	☐ can come	☐ can't come	☐ afternoon	☐ late afternoon
Tony	☐ can come	☐ can't come	☐ afternoon	☐ late afternoon

Pair Check your answers with a partner. Then read Oscar's e-mail message to check your answers.

Oscar's e-mail

Hi, everybody!
   Everybody can come to my house tomorrow afternoon. Yumiko is coming late in the afternoon around 4:00.
   Oscar

2 Where is Oscar's house?

Look at the pictures. Listen to the conversation.

Lynn: I can't find *Oscar's house.* Where is *it?*

Tony: Over there. It's *number 1314.*

Yumiko: Excuse me. I can't find number *1314 Spring Street.*

Neighbor: *1314* is over there.

Yumiko: Oh, thank you.

Pair Practice the conversations. Use your own address.

3 Information Gap Activity, pages 107 and 108.

Turn to pages 107 and 108. Follow your teacher's instructions.

4 Word Bag: *Can*

🔊 Listen. Then listen again and read each sentence aloud.

1.

She can type.

2.

He can cook.

3.

She can swim.

4.

He can drive.

5.

They can dance.

6.

He can play the piano.

7.

He can use a computer.

8.

She can speak English.

I can speak English.

9.

She can play baseball.

🔊 Now listen to the conversation. Then repeat with your teacher.

Can *he cook*?
Yes, *he can*.

Can *she speak English*?
Yes, *she can*.

Pair Work with a partner. Ask and answer questions about the pictures above.

5 They can play the piano.

Under each picture, write a sentence with *can* and an expression from the list below.

use a computer	speak English	drive
play the piano	cook	dance
swim	play baseball	type

1. 
<u>He can use a computer.</u>

2.

3.

4.

5.

6.

7.  *I can speak English.*

8.

9.

6 Can you dance?

Walk around the room. Ask five classmates questions about what they *can* or *can't do*. In the chart below, write each person's name and something he or she can do.

Example: *Can* you *dance*?
Yes, I *can*. (No, I *can't*.)

Name	What He or She Can Do

7 See it. Hear it. Say it.

Read and learn.

The Sound of Long *e*

Long *e* sounds like the *e* in three and seat.

 Listen and repeat.

3		
1. three	2. sheep	3. feet
4. seat	5. meat	6. leaf

CHECKPOINT

I can

- give someone my address.
- ask for someone's address.
- ask and say what someone *can* or *can't* do.
- invite someone.
- ask for help.

VOCABULARY

Time Expressions
tomorrow
tonight

Other
address
can
come
e-mail
identification card (ID)
live
where

Action Verbs
type
cook
swim
drive
dance

play the piano
play baseball
speak English
use a computer

► COMMUNICATION SUMMARY

Expressing ability
Can you dance?
    Yes, I can. No, I can't.

Inviting a person
Can you come to my house tonight?

Accepting or declining an invitation
Yes, I can.
No, I can't.

Negotiating times
No, I can't. How about tomorrow afternoon?
What about tomorrow?

Requesting assistance
I can't find Oscar's house. Where is it?
Excuse me. I can't find number 1314 Spring Street.

Mr. Garcia is in the kitchen.

 Listen. Look at the picture and point to the people.

Listen again and read.

This is Oscar's house. Oscar is welcoming his friends Lynn and Tony at the front door. His sister Stella is washing the car. Mr. Garcia is in the kitchen. He's cooking dinner. Bobby and Maria, Oscar's brother and sister, are setting the table in the dining room.

Mrs. Garcia is using the computer in the living room. There are three bedrooms upstairs. There are two bathrooms, one full bath upstairs and a half-bath downstairs. It's a comfortable home.

What do you think a full bathroom and a half-bath are?

1 Word Bag: The House

📼   Look at the picture on page 66. Point to each room or object as you hear it named. Then listen and repeat.

2 She's in the living room.

Look at the pictures. Write the name of the room or place under the picture.

1. _____

2. _____

3. _____

4. _____

5. _____

6. _____

3 He's cooking dinner.

📼   Look at the pictures above and listen.

Student A: Where's *Mr. Garcia*?

Student B: *He's in the kitchen.*

Student A: What's *he* doing?

Student B: *He's cooking dinner.*

Student A: Where *are Bobby and Maria*?

Student B: *They're in the dining room.*

Student A: What *are they* doing?

Student B: *They're setting the table.*

Pair   Ask and answer questions about what the people in the pictures are doing.

4 We need a stove for the kitchen.

<u>**Pair**</u>   Read the list below and write the name under the picture. Then write the name of each item in a room below.

a medicine cabinet	a dresser	a refrigerator	a bookcase	cabinets
an armchair	a mirror	a bathtub	a table	a bed
a picture	a stove	a sofa	a television	a sink

Living Room	Dining Room	Kitchen	Bedroom	Bathroom

You're moving into a new house. On a piece of paper, make a list of the things you need for each room in your new house. Use words from the list above. You may add more items to your list.

5 There's a car in the garage.

Pair   Look at the picture. Read the names of the items in the house.

car	blinds	books	bookcase	chairs	curtains
flowers	lamp	pictures	rug	shower	cabinet

Complete the sentences.

1. There are _____ in the yard.

2. There are _____ in the kitchen.

3. There's a _____ in the living room. It's green.

4. There are _____ on the table in the living room. There's a _____ on the table too.

5. There are _____ on the windows in the kitchen.

6. There are two _____ on the wall in the bedroom.

7. There's a _____ in the bathroom.

8. There's a _____ in the garage.

6 This is my living room.

Draw a room in your home.

Describe your picture. Write some sentences about it on the lines below. Use *there is* and *there are* where it is appropriate.

_____

_____

_____

_____

_____

_____

_____

_____

7 Are there any flowers in the yard?

🔊 **Listen. Then practice with your teacher.**

Student A: Is there a tree in the yard?

Student B: No, there isn't.

Student A: Is there a rug in the living room?

Student B: Yes, there is.

Student A: Are there any flowers in the yard?

Student B: Yes, there are.

Student A: Are there any curtains in the living room?

Student B: No, there aren't.

Pair Work with a partner. Look again at the picture on page 66. Take turns asking and answering questions about the house.

8 Is it the living room?

🔊 **Listen. Write the name of the room of the house or the place the people are talking about.**

1. _____

2. _____

3. _____

4. _____

5. _____

6. _____

9 Information Gap Activity, pages 109 and 110

Turn to pages 109 and 110. Follow your teacher's instructions.

10 See it. Hear it. Say it.

Read and learn.

The Sound of Long *i*

> Long *i* sounds like the *i* in **pie** and **night**.

Listen and repeat.

1. pie	2. tie	3. knife
4. night	5. light	6. high

CHECKPOINT

I can

- ❑ identify rooms in a house.
- ❑ identify furniture.
- ❑ describe things.
- ❑ describe the location of things.
- ❑ ask what people are doing.
- ❑ tell what people are doing.

VOCABULARY

The Bedroom
a bed
a desk
a dresser
a mirror
a night table
a rug
blinds

The Bathroom
a bathtub
a medicine
  cabinet
a sink

The Kitchen
a refrigerator
a sink
a stove
cabinets

The Dining Room
a table
chairs

The Living Room
a bookcase
a lamp
a picture
a sofa
a stereo
a table
a television (TV)
an armchair
curtains

The Garage
a car

The Yard
a tree
flowers

► COMMUNICATION SUMMARY

Identifying household furniture/rooms and describing their locations
This is my living room. There are two sofas and an armchair in my living room.

Asking about and confirming locations of objects
Is there a tree in the yard?
      Yes, there is.
Are there curtains in the living room?
      No, there aren't.

Telling what someone is doing
He's cooking dinner.
They're setting the table.

Look at the picture. Listen and read the conversation.

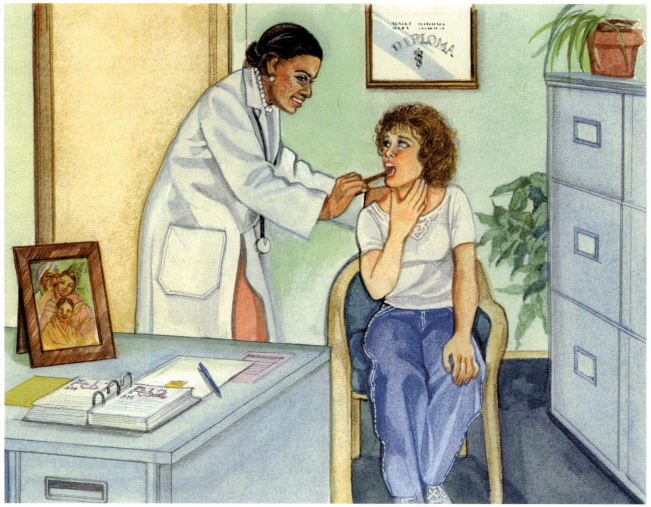

Doctor: How do you feel, Susan?

Susan: I feel terrible.

Doctor: What's the matter?

Susan: I have a sore throat. It hurts.

Doctor: I'm sorry to hear that. Let's take a look. Open your mouth and say, "Aaah."

Susan: Aaah.

Doctor: Your throat is a little red, Susan. It looks swollen, too. I'll give you a prescription. Don't worry. You'll be fine.

Pair Practice the conversation.

1 Word Bag: Parts of the Body

Listen to the words. Point to each body part.

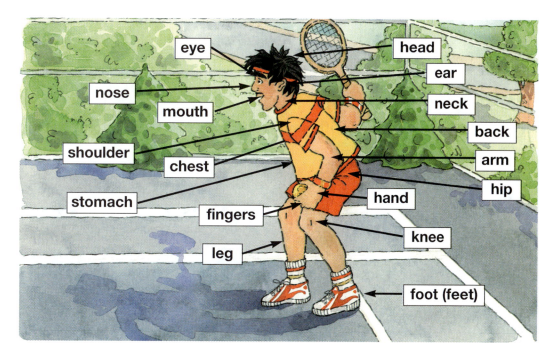

eye

head

nose

ear

mouth

neck

shoulder

back

chest

arm

stomach

hip

fingers

hand

leg

knee

foot (feet)

2 Say, "Aaah."

Listen. Watch as your teacher performs the commands. Listen again and follow each command.

Sit on the table.

Open your mouth.

Say, "Aaah."

Breathe in.

Breathe out.

Roll up your left sleeve.

3 Concentration Game, pages 111 and 112.

Work in groups of three or five. Cut out the word and picture cards on pages 111 and 112. Shuffle the picture cards. Place them, face down, in five rows of four. Do the same for the word cards. Take turns turning over a picture card and a word card. If the two match, read the word, and keep the cards. If the cards don't match, put back the cards, face down. The student with the most pairs of matching cards wins.

4 She has a headache.

🔊 Look at the pictures and read with your teacher. Then listen to the cassette.

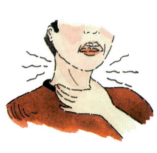

1. Alice
a headache

2. Mary
a backache

3. Betty
a sore throat

4. Hugo
a stomachache

5. Eric
a toothache

6. Ana
a cough

7. Bob
a cold

8. Tim
a fever

🔊 Listen to the conversation.

Student A: What's the matter with *Alice*?
Student B: *She* has a *headache*.
Student A: Does *she* have a *fever*, too?
Student B: No, only a *headache*.

Pair Ask and answer questions about the people in the pictures above.

5 What's the matter?

🔊 **Listen to the conversation.**

Student A:	How are you, *Mia*?	**Student B:**	I have a *headache*.
Student B:	I don't feel very well.	**Student A:**	I'm sorry to hear that.
Student A:	Oh? What's the matter?		

Ask three classmates how they feel. Follow the model. Complete the chart below.

Name	cough	fever	cold	headache	backache	OK
Mia				✓		

Now tell the class. *Mia feels sick. She has a headache.*

6 Please fill out this Patient Information Form.

🔊 **Listen to the conversation twice. Then fill out the information sheet.**

Mᴴ **Mercy Hospital Patient Information**

➤ **Is this your first visit to Dr. Sanders?**
   ___ yes   ___ no

➤ **What is the reason for the visit today?**
   ___ checkup   ___ illness

➤ **Please (✓) all that apply to you.**
   ___ cough   ___ stomachache   ___ allergies
   ___ backache   ___ fever   ___ headache
   ___ sore throat

Pair Check your answers with a partner.

7 Excuses! Excuses!

Pair Read the note from Susan's mother to the teacher.

Dear Ms. Brennan,
I am sorry Susan can't come to school today. She doesn't feel well.
She feels sore all over, and she has a headache and a backache.

Sincerely,

Mrs. R.

What do you understand about Susan?

Check the correct box.

1. ❑ She is going to school today.
   ❑ She is staying home.
   ❑ Susan wrote the note.

2. ❑ She plays sports a lot.
   ❑ She has a cold.
   ❑ She ate bad food.

8 Let's fill out the form for Susan.

Pair Read this form from Mercy Hospital.

Mercy Hospital Patient Information

➤ Is this your first visit to Dr. Sanders? ___ yes   ___ no

➤ Sex   ___ male   ___ female

➤ Age   ___ 0–12 years   ___ 13–25 years
             ___ 26–55 years   ___ 56+ years

➤ What is the reason for coming today?   ___ checkup
                                          ___ sickness

➤ Put a (✓) next to the patient's symptoms.
   ___ chest pain   ___ fever   ___ headaches
   ___ cough   ___ sore throat   ___ back pain
   ___ stomachache   ___ breathing problem

Look at the note above from Susan's mother. On the information form, put a (✔) before each item that describes Susan's problem.

Your brother or sister is not feeling well today. On a piece of paper, write a note to the teacher. Tell him/her that your brother or sister can't come to class and explain why.

9 See it. Hear it. Say it.

Read and learn.

The Sound of Long o

Long o sounds like the o in **coat**.

Listen and repeat.

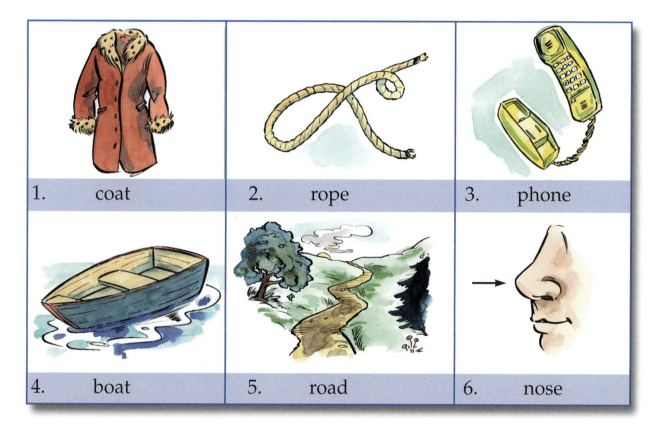

1. coat   2. rope   3. phone

4. boat   5. road   6. nose

CHECKPOINT ✔

I can

❑ identify parts of the body.

❑ indicate areas of pain.

❑ ask how others feel and respond to questions about how I feel.

❑ offer sympathy.

❑ respond to commands and questions from a doctor or a nurse.

❑ fill out and sign forms.

❑ express state of being.

VOCABULARY

Body Parts

arm	leg	foot (feet)
back	mouth	hip
chest	neck	hand
ear	nose	knee
eye	shoulder	
finger	stomach	
head		

Illnesses

allergies
a cold/catch a cold
a cough
a cut
a fever
a headache
a sore throat
a stomachache
a toothache

▶ COMMUNICATION SUMMARY

Asking how someone feels
What's the matter?
How are you?
How do you feel?
What's wrong?
Does she have a fever, too?

Reporting physical states
I have a cold/flu/a stomachache.
I feel terrible.
My throat hurts.
She has a headache.
Mia feels sick.
I don't feel very well.

Offering sympathy
I'm sorry to hear that.
Don't worry. You'll be fine.

Responding to commands and questions from a doctor or nurse
Open your mouth.
Breathe in/Breathe out.
Roll up your left sleeve.

Colors and Clothes

Bring a sweater!

 Listen to the conversation.

Yumiko:	It's very cold in Chicago in January.
Susan:	Yes, it is. Do I need my red sweater?
Yumiko:	Yes, and your blue jacket, too.
Susan:	I don't like that jacket. I'll take my black winter coat.
Yumiko:	Hmm. You need another suitcase. Here, take this one.
Susan:	Thanks! (*Phone rings. Susan answers.*) It's Mark. He's going to Florida.
Yumiko:	Mark's lucky. It's warm and sunny in Florida even in winter.

1 Word Bag: Clothes and Colors

Look at the pictures and read the clothing words and colors with your teacher.

Colors and Clothes

red shorts

a yellow skirt

a pink blouse

a white T-shirt

green socks

white pants

blue jeans

a purple swimsuit

stockings

white tennis shoes

a yellow coat

a green jacket

a brown shirt

black shoes

orange socks

gray pants

a yellow tie

a red scarf

a blue sweater

a black jacket

a navy blue suit

Listen and point to the correct picture.

2 We need clothes for every season.

Draw a line to connect each picture with its name and color.

1. purple skirt
2. pink blouse
3. gray pants
4. white shirt
5. black coat
6. red sweater
7. brown shorts
8. blue jeans
9. green socks
10. orange jacket

Group   Work in a group of three. Put each student's name at the top of the chart and list what that person is wearing under each name.

3 Concentration Game, pages 113 and 114.

Work in groups of three or five. Cut out the word and picture cards on pages 113 and 114. Shuffle the picture cards. Place them, face down, in five rows of four. Do the same for the word cards. Take turns turning over a picture card and a word card. If the two match, read the word, and keep the cards. If the cards don't match, put back the cards, face down. The student with the most pairs of matching cards wins.

4 His or hers?

Pair From the list on the left, complete the chart with the names of clothes that Mark and Susan will pack for their trips.

sweater
dress
suit
shoes
skirt
blouse
tie
scarf
socks
jacket
shirt
pants

Mark	Susan	Both
		shoes

Add three more words to each list.

5 It's cold in New York in the winter.

Look at the pictures as you listen. Complete the sentences with the correct words.

spring	summer	fall	winter
cool	hot, warm	cool	cold

1. It's cold in New York in _____.

2. It's hot and sunny in New York in _____.

3. In New York, flowers bloom in _____.

4. In New York, the leaves turn colors in _____.

Tell the class about the weather in your hometown.

6 Let's buy some new clothes.

Lynn is ordering new clothing for the warm weather. Listen to the dialog. Fill out the order form. Write the name and color of each item and circle the correct size. Then fill in the quantity and price, and add up the total.

His and Hers Catalog Order Form

Item Name and Number	Color	Size	Number of Items × Price	Total
Shorts #321	black	⑤ – 7 – 9	2 × $12.99	$25.98
#832		S – M – L	1 × $39.99	
#944		S – M – L	2 × $19.99	
#157		5 – 7 – 9	1 × $59.95	
#222		S – M – L	3 × $7.00	
			Total	_____

Pair   You're going to the beach on vacation. Shop for new clothes for yourself. Your partner will help you shop. Choose from the items on page 82. Include the colors you want and your sizes.

His and Hers Catalog Order Form

Item Name	Color	Size	Number of Items × Price	Total
			Total	_____

7 Gina is looking good.

Look at Gina's new outfit. What is she wearing? What is everyone else wearing?

1. Susan is wearing _____ _____ shorts, a _____ T-shirt and _____ shoes.

2. Gina is wearing blue _____, a _____ blouse, and brown _____. She is also wearing a pink _____.

3. Oscar is wearing _____ pants, white _____, and a _____ T-shirt.

4. Yumiko is wearing pink _____, a _____ T-shirt, and _____ shoes.

8 You look pretty in pink.

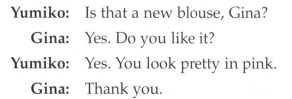 **Look at the pictures. Listen to the conversations.**

Yumiko: Is that a new blouse, Gina?

Gina: Yes. Do you like it?

Yumiko: Yes. You look pretty in pink.

Gina: Thank you.

Yumiko: That's a great picture of you, Oscar. You're very handsome.

Oscar: Thanks, Yumiko.

Pair   Find a partner. Use the examples on page 86 to complete the conversation between Yumiko and Susan.

Yumiko: This is a _____ picture of you. You look beautiful in _____.

Susan: Thanks, Yumiko.

Use the examples above. Go around the room and compliment three people.

9 What can Oscar wear to the party?

Pair   Look at the clothes below and choose outfits for Oscar, Lynn, Yumiko, and Tony.

Oscar can wear _____, _____, _____, and _____.

Lynn can wear _____, _____, _____, and _____.

Yumiko can wear _____, _____, _____, and _____.

Tony can wear _____, _____, _____, and _____.

10 See it. Hear it. Say it.

Read and learn.

The Sound of Long *u*

> **Long *u* sounds like the *u* in blue or suit.**

🎧 **Listen and repeat.**

1. blue	2. glue	3. flu
4. suit	5. fruit	6. juice

CHECKPOINT

I can

❑ describe what one is wearing.

❑ talk about the seasons and the weather.

❑ identify clothes by their name and color.

❑ ask for and make a suggestion.

❑ compliment a person.

❑ acknowledge a compliment.

VOCABULARY

Clothes
blouse
coat
dress
jacket
jeans
pants
scarf
shirt

shorts
shoes
skirt
socks
stockings
suit
sweater
swimsuit
tie

Colors
black
blue
brown
gray
green
orange

pink
purple
red
white
yellow

Action Words
bring
take
wear

Adjectives
beautiful
cold
cool
handsome
hot
pretty
warm

Seasons
autumn/fall
spring
summer
winter

Other
suitcase
trip
vacation
weather

▶ COMMUNICATION SUMMARY

Describing what one is wearing
It's a red sweater.
They're brown pants.

Describing the seasons and the weather
It's very cold in Chicago in January.

Requesting and making a suggestion
Do I need my red sweater?
    Yes, and your blue jacket, too.
What can Oscar wear?
    Oscar can wear _____.

Giving and acknowledging a compliment
I like your shirt.
    Thanks. Thank you.
You're very handsome.
You look pretty in pink.
    Thanks.

UNIT 12
Review of Units 7-11

▶ Topics

Clothing
Food
Shopping
U.S. currency/prices
Rooms of a house
Daily activities
Parts of the body
Illnesses
Visiting the doctor
The seasons
Weather

▶ Communication Summary

Identifying U.S. coins and bills by name and value
Adding up money
Reading ads
Identifying rooms in a house
Identifying furniture
Asking and telling what people can do
Identifying parts of the body
Indicating areas of pain
Expressing how someone feels
Discussing what someone is wearing
Talking about the seasons and the weather
Identifying clothes by name and color

Review

There's a sale on sweaters!

 Look at the pictures. Then listen.

Lynn:	That's a nice sweater, Yumiko.		**Lynn:**	I need a new sweater, too.
Yumiko:	Do you like it?		**Yumiko:**	Well, there's a sale on sweaters at the Lady Bug today. You can buy one there.
Lynn:	Yes, you look pretty in blue.		**Lynn:**	Great! Let's go.
Yumiko:	Thank you.			

Tell the class about a great sale you know about.

1 How much money do you have?

Pair Read the money below. Write the value of each kind of money. Add up the total for each list.

Coins	Number	Value		Bills	Number	Value
pennies	6	$0.06		ones	2	$2.00
nickels	1			fives	2	
dimes	1			tens	1	
quarters	1			twenties	2	
half-dollars	1			fifties	1	
Total	10			**Total**	8	

2 Oscar's going shopping.

Pair Look at the ad. Write the prices on Oscar's shopping list. Add up the total.

SPEEDY MART   BIG SALE!   This Week Only

Apples 79¢ a pound   Bananas 30¢ a pound   Grapes $1.99 a pound   Cake $3.50   Milk $2.50 a gallon   White Bread 90¢ a loaf   Ice Cream $6.00 a gallon

Oscar's Shopping List

2 pounds of apples   _____

1 gallon of milk   _____

2 loaves of bread   _____

3 pounds of grapes   _____

1/2 gallon of ice cream   _____

_____

Total

3 Home sweet home!

Group Work in groups of three. Look at the picture. On a piece of paper, write the names of the rooms and objects that you see in the house.

Read your list to the class. Which group has the most words?

4 Find someone who can play the piano.

Group Work in groups of five. Ask the members of your group the following questions. Check *Yes*, *No*, or *A Little*.

Can you . . .	Yes	No	A Little
1. play the piano?	_____	_____	_____
2. use a computer?	_____	_____	_____
3. drive a car?	_____	_____	_____
4. play tennis?	_____	_____	_____
5. swim?	_____	_____	_____

Share the information with the class.

1. _____ members (member) can play the piano.
2. _____ can use a computer.
3. _____ can drive a car.
4. _____ can play tennis.
5. _____ can swim.

5 Body Parts

Group Label the body parts on the lines provided.

ear	back	knee
neck	eye	stomach
arm	hip	chest
head	shoulder	foot
nose	finger	leg
		mouth

6 What's the matter?

1. Jack

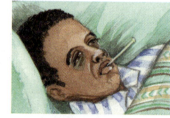
2. Eric

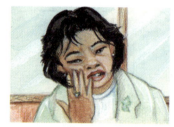
3. Naomi

4. Mr. Andrews

5. Myra

6. Margo

Pair Look at the pictures above. Ask a partner what he or she thinks is the matter with each person.

Example:

Student A: What's the matter with *Jack?*

Student B: *He has a cold.*

7 Let's make a class journal.

Pair Work with a partner. Ask the following questions.

Student Questionnaire

1. What day is today?
2. Name three things you are wearing.
3. What color are your shoes?
4. What is your favorite color?
5. What do you like to wear in spring?
6. What do you like to wear in summer?
7. What do you like to wear in fall?
8. What do you like to wear in winter?
9. What do you like to wear to school?
10. What do you like to wear to a party?

Write about your partner.

⋯⋯⋯Journal⋯⋯⋯

_____
[1]

    I am in my English class. My partner is wearing _____, _____,
[2]
and _____ today. Her/(His) shoes are _____. Her/(His) favorite
[3]
color is _____. She/(He) likes to wear _____ in the spring.
[4]   [5]
She/(He) likes to wear _____ in the summer. She/(He) likes to wear
[6]
_____ in the fall. She/(He) likes to wear _____ in the winter.
[7]   [8]
    She/(He) likes to wear _____ to school and _____ to a
[9]   [10]
party.

Read the paragraphs to the class.

8 Guess what the weather is.

Class Activity

1. **Think** of a weather condition.
2. **Write** the weather condition on a piece of paper.
3. **Fold** the paper.
4. **Put** your folded paper in a box on the teacher's table.
5. **Take turns** taking a folded paper from the box.
6. **Read** the weather condition.
7. **Act out** the weather condition.
8. Class: **Guess** what the weather condition is.

9 We have clothes for every season.

Pair   Match the clothes to the season.

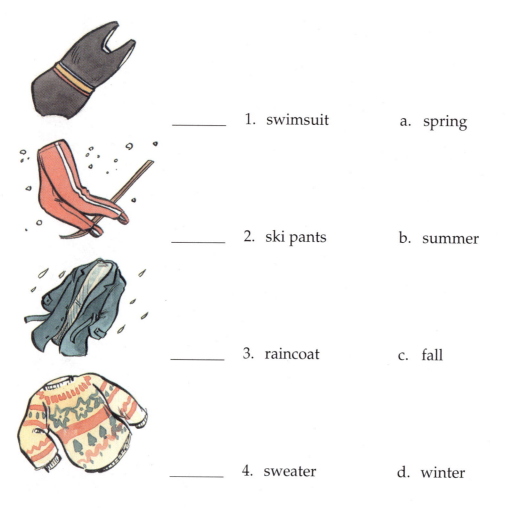

_____ 1. swimsuit   a. spring

_____ 2. ski pants   b. summer

_____ 3. raincoat   c. fall

_____ 4. sweater   d. winter

► GAMES AND ACTIVITIES

Sentence Puzzle

Hello.	I'm	Oscar.
is	Tony.	It's
you.	Nice	to
Hi,	Lynn.	How
fine,	thank	you.
thanks.	Good	morning.
evening.	Good-bye.	Good
tomorrow.	My	name
Hi.	to	meet
nice	you,	too.
meet	you?	I'm
are	night.	Fine,
And	afternoon.	Good
Good	See	you

Alphabet Game

Concentration Game

bookshelf	door	pencil sharpener	chair
chalkboard	dictionary	globe	notebook
eraser	chalk	computer	clock
file cabinet	pencil	window	desk

Concentration Game

© 1998 Prentice Hall Regents. Duplication for classroom use is permitted.

Information Gap Activity

Student A

Look at the chart below. Some information is missing. Ask your partner for the missing information, and write it in the chart. Don't look at your partner's chart!

Name	Age	Height	Hair	Eyes
Al Romo	23		short curly	
Ann Baker		tall		blue
Susan Wong	52	average	long black	
Jack Mishubi				dark brown
Alice Sage	24	short	short blonde	
Masoud Shafiem				green

Useful Language

How old is *Ann Baker/Jack Mishubi?*
What color is *his/her* hair?
What color are *his/her* eyes?
Is *he/she* short/tall?

Information Gap Activity  Student B

Look at the chart below. Some information is missing. Ask your partner for the missing information, and write it in the chart. Don't look at your partner's chart!

Name	Age	Height	Hair	Eyes
Al Romo		short		gray
Ann Baker	37		curly red	
Susan Wong				brown
Jack Mishubi	61	average	bald	
Alice Sage				dark blue
Masoud Shafiem	22	tall	black	

Useful Language

How old is *Al Romo/Susan Wong?*
What color is *his/her hair?*
What color are *his/her eyes?*
Is *he/she short/tall?*

Information Gap Activity

A.1 Look at the clock faces. Ask your partner: "What time is it?" Draw the hands on the clocks.

a.

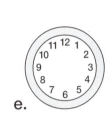

b.

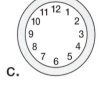

c.

d.

e.

f.

g.

h.

i.

A.2 Look at the clock. Tell your partner the time.

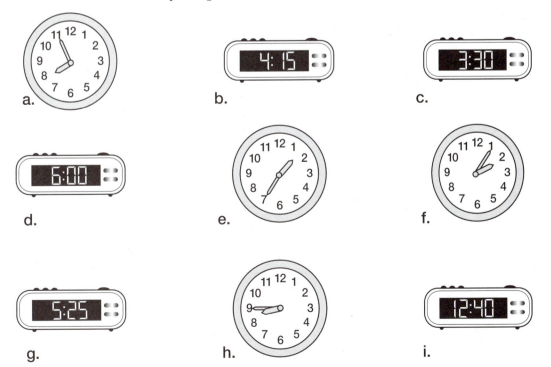

a.

b.

c.

d.

e.

f.

g.

h.

i.

Information Gap Activity

B.1 Look at the clocks. Tell your partner the time.

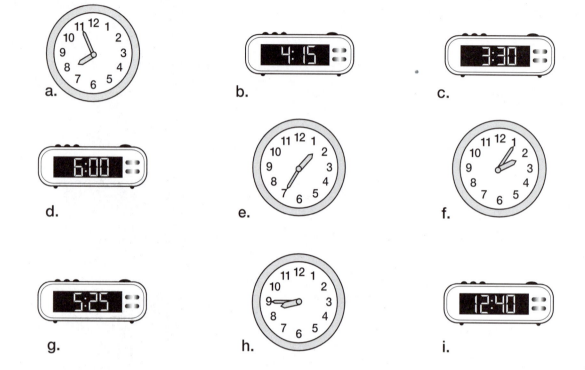

a.

b.

c.

d.

e.

f.

g.

h.

i.

B.2 Look at the clock faces. Ask your partner: "What time is it?" Draw the hands on the clocks.

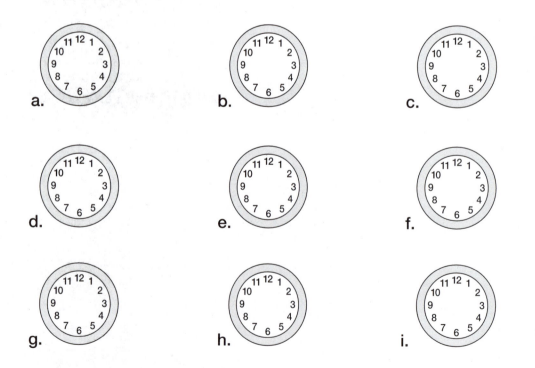

a.

b.

c.

d.

e.

f.

g.

h.

i.

Information Gap Activity

Student A

1. Look at the prices. Ask your partner: "How much is it?"

Listen to your partner. Circle the price you hear.

a. $0.15	$0.50	$50.00
b. $30.00	$13.00	$33.00
c. $44.40	$44.14	$40.04
d. $1.72	$1.12	$1.02
e. $60.66	$16.66	$66.66

2. Look at the prices. Tell your partner the prices.

a. $0.50
b. $13.00
c. $40.04
d. $1.12
e. $66.66

1. Look at the prices. Tell your partner the prices.

a. $0.15
b. $33.00
c. $44.14
d. $1.12
e. $16.66

2. Look at the prices. Ask your partner: "How much is it?"

Listen to your partner. Circle the price you hear.

a. $0.15	$0.50	$50.00
b. $30.00	$13.00	$33.00
c. $44.40	$44.14	$40.04
d. $1.72	$1.12	$1.02
e. $60.66	$16.66	$66.66

Information Gap Activity 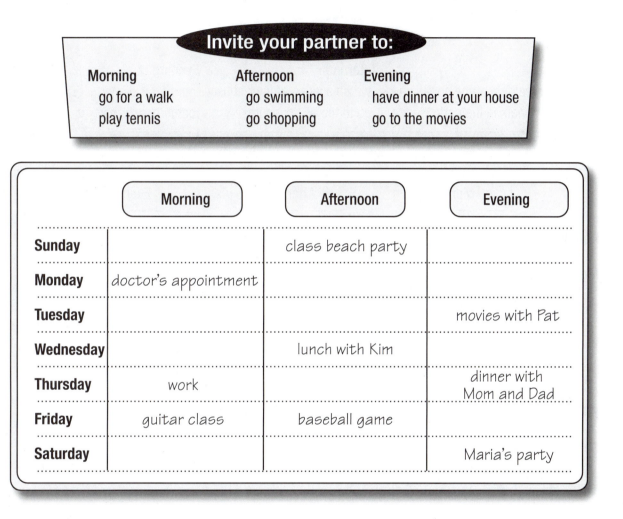 Student A

Look at your schedule for next week. Invite your partner to do the things mentioned in the list. Write the appointments you make in your schedule. Don't look at your partner's page.

Invite your partner to:

Morning	Afternoon	Evening
go for a walk	go swimming	have dinner at your house
play tennis	go shopping	go to the movies

	Morning	Afternoon	Evening
Sunday		class beach party	
Monday	doctor's appointment		
Tuesday			movies with Pat
Wednesday		lunch with Kim	
Thursday	work		dinner with Mom and Dad
Friday	guitar class	baseball game	
Saturday			Maria's party

Useful Language
Can you go for a walk on *Sunday morning?*
Yes, I can.
No, I can't. How about on *Wednesday morning?*

Information Gap Activity

Look at your schedule for next week. Invite your partner to do the things mentioned in the list. Write the appointments you make in your schedule. Don't look at your partner's page.

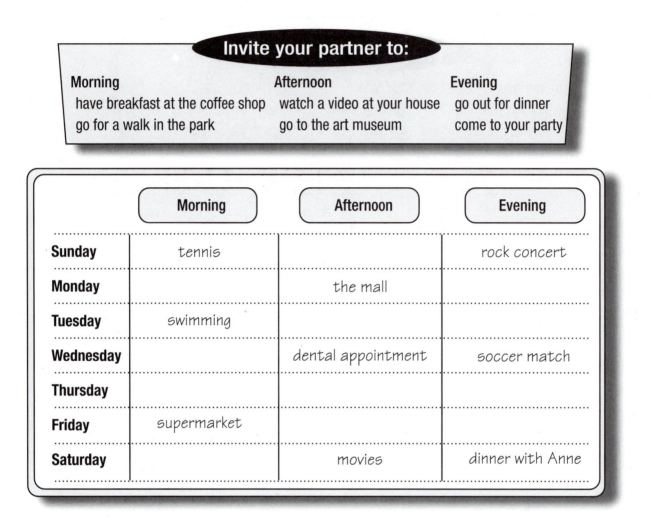

Invite your partner to:

Morning
have breakfast at the coffee shop
go for a walk in the park

Afternoon
watch a video at your house
go to the art museum

Evening
go out for dinner
come to your party

	Morning	Afternoon	Evening
Sunday	tennis		rock concert
Monday		the mall	
Tuesday	swimming		
Wednesday		dental appointment	soccer match
Thursday			
Friday	supermarket		
Saturday		movies	dinner with Anne

Useful Language
Can you have breakfast at the
  coffee shop *Monday morning*?
Sure, I can.
No, I can't. How about on
  Wednesday morning?

Information Gap Activity

Student A

Look at the picture. Your partner has a picture of the same house with seven differences. Ask each other questions to find the differences. Mark the differences on your picture. Don't look at your partner's picture.

Useful Language

Is there a *woman* in the *bedroom*?
Yes, *there is.* No, *there isn't?*
There's a *woman in the kitchen.*
What's the *woman* doing?
He's/She's cooking.
Where is the *woman*?

Look at the picture. Your partner has a picture of the same house with seven differences. Find the differences. Ask each other questions to find the differences. Mark the differences on your picture. Don't look at your partner's picture.

Useful Language

Is there a *woman* in the *bedroom*?
Yes, *there is*. No, *there isn't*?
There's a *woman* in the *kitchen*.
What's the *woman* doing?
He's/She's cooking.
Where is the *woman*?

Concentration Game

back	head	stomach	hand
eye	tooth	leg	knee
foot	finger	arm	mouth
ear	nose	shoulder	neck

Concentration Game

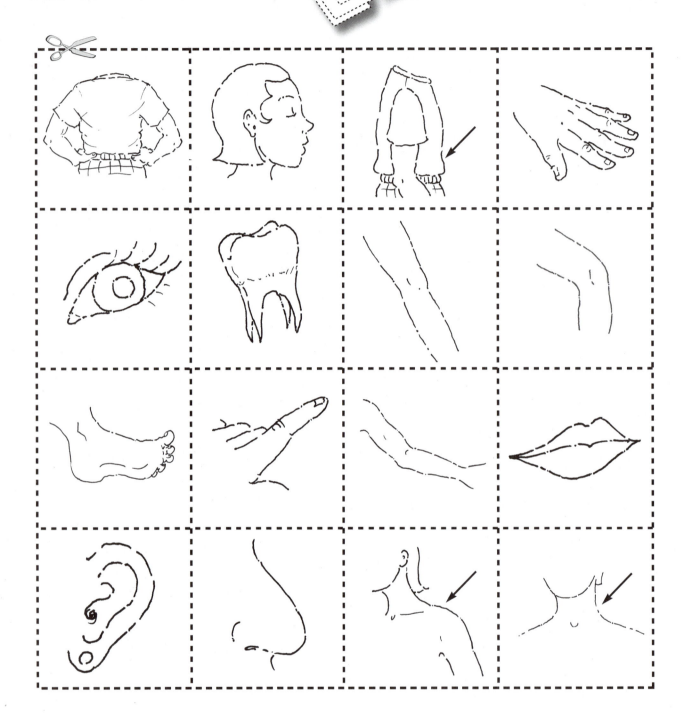

Concentration Game

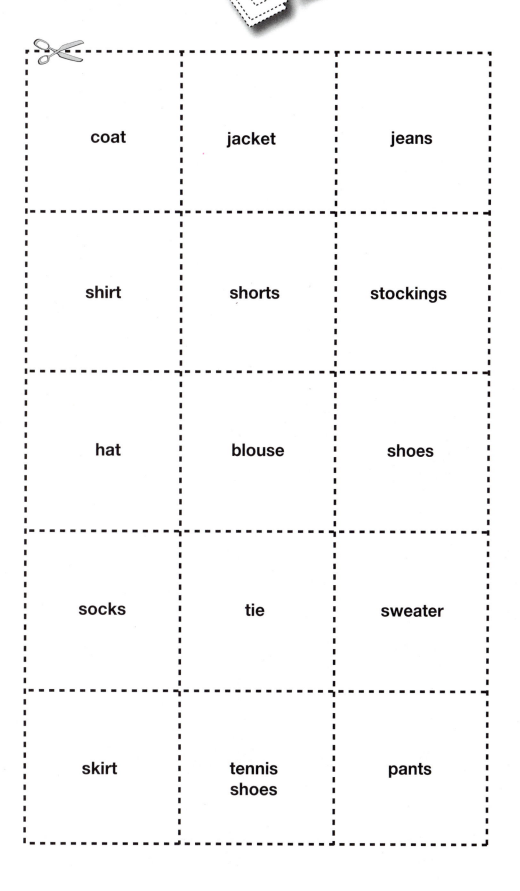

coat	jacket	jeans
shirt	shorts	stockings
hat	blouse	shoes
socks	tie	sweater
skirt	tennis shoes	pants

Concentration Game